Theorising Development in Africa:
Towards Building an African Framework of Development

Munyaradzi Mawere

Langaa Research & Publishing CIG
Mankon, Bamenda

Publisher
Langaa RPCIG
Langaa Research & Publishing Common Initiative Group
P.O. Box 902 Mankon
Bamenda
North West Region
Cameroon
Langaagrp@gmail.com
www.langaa-rpcig.net

Distributed in and outside N. America by African Books Collective
orders@africanbookscollective.com
www.africanbookscollective.com

ISBN-10: 9956-764-74-4

ISBN-13: 978-9956-764-74-7

© Munyaradzi Mawere 2017

All rights reserved.
No part of this book may be reproduced or transmitted in any form or by any means, mechanical or electronic, including photocopying and recording, or be stored in any information storage or retrieval system, without written permission from the publisher

Table of Contents

Chapter 1
What Development Is and Is Not........................ 1

Chapter 2
Development and Underdevelopment
in Africa: Through the Lenses of Theory.............. 23

Chapter 3
The Blame Game and Politics of
Development in Africa..................................... 59

Chapter 4
Development, Underdevelopment and
Globalisation in Africa.................................... 75

Chapter 5
Poverty and Inequality: Unpacking
the Pragmatics of Poverty and
Inequality in Africa...95

Chapter 6
Development, Agriculture and
the Diffusion of Technology in
Rural Africa..117

Chapter 7
Gender and Development in Africa.................... 125

Chapter 8
Social Policy and Development in Africa………….. 137

Chapter 9
Climate Change and Environmental
Management Strategies in Africa…......................... 151

Chapter 10
Building Blocks of Development:
Towards a Framework of Development
for Africa……………………………………………...167

References……………………………………… 179

Chapter 1

What Development Is and Is Not

> *"Development is not all about building roads, schools, hospitals and towns. It is what we qualitatively do with the roads, the schools, the hospitals and the towns we build. It is not only about the quantities of what is built, but what people benefit from all that is built for them and others to come" (Munyaradzi Mawere 2016).*

Introduction: Theory and development in Africa

While there are many theories and models of development that have been used (and continue to be used) in Africa even today – from modernisation to integration and globalisation theories of development – most if not all of these theories have been developed either in Europe or the Americas? One then wonders if these theories and models, no matter how strong they might be, could be wholesomely applicable to contexts such as Africa which are different from those of the places and people they were developed. Two questions that come to mind thus are: To what extend can the theories developed in the Global North be applicable to Africa? Why is it that we seem to lack development theories and models from Africa and for Africa?

In reflecting critically on the first question, one notes that most of the theories and models imported from the Global North are either useless or limited when it comes to contexts such as those of Africa. They are limited because they principally reflect the thinking and the objectives of those who coin them together with their unique circumstances and experiences. This calls for the scholars and theorists of development in Africa to be very swift and meticulous in their theorisation and contribution to development discourse, particularly with regard to Africa. On this note, I argue that "development for conquest" that the Europe and the Americas have imposed (consciously or unconsciously) on the indigenous people of Africa must be substituted by a development paradigm that celebrates their creative and innovative potentials while also recognising their contribution to the global stock of development.

Similarly, a critical reflection on the second question reveals that there are a number of factors that have caused Africa to be gullible of all the models and theories – even if they are worst – and bluntly deploy in their contexts. Two factors at the fore are colonialism and colonial education which denied the African people not only their humanity as a people but also their creative and innovative geniuses as well as their right to equally contribute to the global mantra of development. As Santos, Nunes and Meneses argue (2007: xxxiii):

> This denial of diversity is a constitutive and persistent feature of colonialism. While the political dimension of colonial intervention has been widely criticised, the burden of the colonial epistemic monoculture is still accepted nowadays as a symbol of development and modernity.

It is worth noting that the colonists inquisitively considered themselves as the "all knowers" and legitimate producers of all knowledge and development theories and models that unquestionably deserves transcultural application and acceptance. No wonder Santos, Nunes and Meneses (Ibid: xix) had this to say of the imposed Western supremacy on Africa:

> the epistemological privilege granted to modern science from the seventeenth century onwards, which made possible the technological revolutions that consolidated Western supremacy, was also instrumental in suppressing other, non-scientific forms of knowledges and, at the same time, the subaltern social groups whose social practices were informed by such knowledges.

The horrendous and atrocious forces of colonialism and colonial education saw Africa being negatively described in mass media and by some theorists of the North as a continent characterised by social chaos, political instability, abject poverty, social unrest, civil wars, and diseases. A manifold question can, however, be raised in view of this characterisation: How far true are these characterisations? Isn't it that Africa is more than this characterisation and certainly different from the negative image portrayed in some circles? Isn't it from Africa that we had the cradle of civilisation in pre-colonial era? Isn't it from Africa that we get cultural, philosophical, and spiritual diversity with great potentials to contribute to global peace and justice? Isn't it in Africa where we have a long history of successful struggle against colonialism and human exploitation? Isn't it in Africa where we find the rich deposits of minerals, flourishing forests, wildlife, mountains and rivers? In fact, as Lamb (1983:20) reminds us:

> 40% of the world's potential hydroelectric power supply; the bulk of the world's diamonds …; 30% of the uranium in the non-communist world; 50% of the world's gold; 90% of its cobalt; 50% of its phosphates; … 7.5% of its coal; … 3% of its iron ore; and millions upon millions of acres of untilled farmland […] Africa has 60% of the world's cultivatable land. Arguably, there is no other continent blessed with such abundance and diversity.

Scholars like Kaberuka (2013) add that:

> Africa has more than 122 billion barrels of proven oil reserves (13% of world's oil), 500 trillion cubic feet of gas reserves (12% of global gas) and 90% of chromium and platinum group metals; 20% of the world's copper and significant deposits of bauxite, tantalum and other minerals. In addition, it has 64% of the world's manganese, and vast nickel, lead, tungsten and cobalt; rutile (titanium ore), emeralds, lithium and tin (p.3).

In addition to the above, Ayittey (1999: 6), notes that Africa also accounts for "70% of cocoa, 60% of coffee, 50% of palm oil, and

20% of the total petroleum traded in the world market, excluding the United States and Russia."

If it is indeed the case that Africa is blooming with all the riches mentioned in my question above, why then do Africa's doomsters contradict this logic? Is there any spite and scheming against Africa that is possibly inspired by the quest of the Global North[1] to exploit Africa forever as it has done before national independence? By what and whose measurement is Africa characterised as such? From this critical questioning, it is at least clear that the question whether Africa is truly underdeveloped or not is more of a dichotomous matter that needs to be looked at from both sides of the coin. It is not a question to approach from a monolithic view point. At another level, questions that continue troubling us are: With all its richness in natural resources and human capital of quality and strength, how can Africa contribute meaningfully to global development, especially in a world that is dominated by hegemonic narratives of the North? How could Africa's contribution help resolve the social and environmental ills, eliminate the political and economic traumas, and eradicate the laden sprouts of civil unrest on the continent and the global world? And lastly, what exactly can be labelled as "real" development given that many theories from the North and their attendant forces of change such as capitalism, colonialism, neo-colonialism and globalisation, which all came in the guise of civilisation and development, have arguably inflicted untold sufferings and agony to the societies of the South? In fact, there is need to trouble the concept and conceptualisation of [under-]development before we

---

[1] While I acknowledge that the Western scholars have come to label the Africans as the "Global South," even without acknowledging the pillaging and plundering done during slave trade and colonialism, I emphasise here that in this book I use the terms "Global South" and "Global North" neutrally to mean Africa (and all other continents in the southern hemisphere that suffered colonialism) and the countries in the northern hemisphere (including North America) that participated in the enslavement and colonisation of Africa. I thus use the terms "Global South" and "Global North" chiefly with respect to their geographical locations and their respective roles and positions during colonialism. Also, sometimes I use the terms North and South to refer to the Global North and Global South respectively.

seek solutions to come out of its box. It needs to be written in bold that while the idea of development as applied to Africa presupposes that Africa's major problem is lack of development, the truth is that Africa's primary predicament is one of continual exploitation and looting of its resources – natural and human of quality – by the capitalist imperialists of the Global North, who in most either connive (explicitly or implicitly) with the African elite or do so forcibly through their lopsided draconian so-called international laws. Also, it needs to be said loud and clear that by emphasising on matters of poverty, the idea of development presupposes that Africa's major problem is simply that of poverty when in actual fact the prime problem that Africa has suffered and continue to suffer even today is that of pillaging or exploitation of its precious resources, denial of compensation from by its former colonisers, privileging business entrepreneurs from the Global North at the expense of those from the South, continued machinations and scheming through the deployment of such forces as globalisation, robbery, and looting. This presupposition sadly conceals and sweeps under carpet the real problem that haunts Africa. It also diverts attention of committed African theorists and development practitioners on the real problem that Africa faces, making it even more difficult to find enduring solutions.

It is indeed in the light of this background and critical reflection that the quotation above was formulated. The quotation was adopted from a vignette by one of my interlocutors during fieldwork in southern Zimbabwe in 2011. It troubles and teases out the conceptualisation and traditional definition of development as inclined towards materiality and poverty-related issues. Most importantly, the vignette clearly depicts that the term "development" though has gained tremendous prominence in intellectual discourse over the years in both Africa and beyond, remains peculiarly difficult to unpack and define with precision. This is chiefly because, on one hand, the term is elastic and pragmatic such that it cuts across contexts and life situations and, on the other hand, it means different things to different people. In fact, it should be underlined that development like all socially constructed notions is highly elusive and unstable. Given the nebulous nature coupled with the different interpretations of development, a robust comprehension of term calls into question its practical manifestations and applications in particular situated contexts, particularly those of the so-called developing economies such as Africa. That said, this chapter seeks to unpack what development is and is not in view of scholars such as Todaro, Swanepoel, Nyerere, Sen, Seers, Rodney, Chambers, Easterlin, Mabogunje, and Peet and Hartwick, among many others. In this attempt the chapter simultaneously unpacks the ambiguities associated with the term "development" and discusses the assertion whether development is all about making life better for all people concerned.

Conceptualising development

As highlighted above, the term "development" and the discourse surrounding it is highly momentous and has sustained controversies of epic proportions in both theory and practice such that scholars like Thomas (2004: 1-2) has observed that development is "a concept which is contested both theoretically and politically, and is inherently both complex and ambiguous." In some contexts, the meaning of development has been often assumed, taken for granted, loosely and uncritically applied while in others development has been described with caution and criticality. This has resulted in lack of agreement over what development really is and what its goals should be. Subsequently, development has assumed different definitions and interpretations with scholars such as Swanepoel (2011: xv) arguing that "the concept of development has suffered much abuse over the last fifty years". The same realisation has prompted scholars such as Musingafi *et al* (2013) to observe that some scholars have limited development to material wealth and others to liberty and spiritual progress, whereas more others despise it as a product of neo-colonialism. In fact, since, at least the writings of Adam Smith in his: *The Wealth of Nations*, the notion of development has been closely linked or rather identified with the idea of economic growth. In this sense, development has, more often than not, been thought of by very few modern economists (and other social scientists alike) as something that mean more than economy. Yet, what Adam Smith sought to promote and enlighten was the attainment of economic growth in pursuit of what he understood as "the wealth of nations." It is for this major reason that Smith (1776: 446) argued that the capital that had been "silently and gradually accumulated by the private frugality and good conduct of individuals, by their universal, continual, and uninterrupted effort to better their own condition had maintained the progress of England towards opulence and improvement" (Smith 1776/1977: 446). This, in turn, led to the "improvement, in the productive powers of labour which allowed more and more people to enjoy a greater share of the necessaries and conveniences of life in the civilised and thriving nations as contrasted to the savage nations of hunters and fishers" (Smith 1776: 104-105). As could be seen, Smith's conception of development was narrow and limited to economics.

From all these different conceptualisations of development, a plethora of definitions and approaches have been conjured throughout history basing on one's orientation. The conception of development that was more prevalent in the economic literature of the early post-Second World War period, for example, remained that development is equal to economic growth. In fact, when the idea of 'development' emerged in the second half of the twentieth century, it was traditionally interpreted as 'economic growth' which is measured by per capita income and average annual growth in national income (World Bank 1980). This understanding was prevalent chiefly because the economic focus of development in the 1950s and 1960s was a vision of liberating people, through structural transformation (Gore 2000). This 'growth-based' understanding of development, according to Sant'Ana (2008), was premised on the idea that growth of the economy would benefit the whole society, either by market-driven 'trickle down' effects, or by state-driven social policy. Yet as Gyekye (2013) rightly tells us, this Western epistemological paradigm which sees economic thinking in terms of exaggerated emphasis on quantitative indexes of wealth and identification of economic development with the capacity of national economy to generate accumulative gross national product of above 5%, does not apply to contexts such as those of Africa. These principles and categories of Western epistemological paradigm which Gyekye describes as "economism" undermines the values and knowledge system that sustain African indigenous economic organisation (p. 29-30). In fact, as far as development in Africa and indeed the conceptualisation development as multi-dimensional is concerned, Gyekye sees economism as misplaced, limiting, and narrow focused given that it overlooks historical, cultural and economic situations in the philosophical conception of economic development. As Gyekye explains, economism falsely categorises people into classes of wealthy and poor, and developed and underdeveloped; categories that are misleading in the African economic worldview. Thus, applying such categories to Africa remains more of a misnomer to the extent that Gyekye perceives the divisions as false because they leave out a third category of 'average wealth' and 'developing' in each category respectively. For this major reason, Gyekye reason that economism is lopsided, inadequate and unrealistic as it fails to accommodate the complexities of human nature, society and culture. Gyekye does not mince his words in view of these categories as he argues: "economism is fallacious because it identifies economic development with development yet a species cannot be identical with its genus" (Gyekye 2013: 30). Such unrealistic assumptions, the narrowness and fallacious understanding of development as exposed by Gyekye justifies the need for an African Philosophy of development that informatively and meaningfully accommodates the African framework, historical, cultural and economic circumstances.

Subscribing to the 'growth-based development' camp, the Economist, Richard Easterlin (1968: 395), has come to conceive development as "a rapid and sustained rise in real output per head and attendant shifts in the technological, economic, and demographic characteristics of a society." While this interpretation of development is appealing especially from a developed societies' perspective where real output per head rises on a self-sustained basis with certain advancements "in technology and reduction of dependents each individual has to support, in practice, this interpretation is only applicable in a gross, macro-structural sense in which the role of the individuals involved in the process become completely unimportant compared to the total commodity produced and the proportion put aside as savings for further investment" (Mabogunje 1980: 36). Besides, it can be argued that such conception of development as economic growth is excessively narrow given that it confines development to quantitative betterment while leaving aside other important dimensions associated with "sustainability" and "good or better human life" such as the psychological, spiritual, environmental, cultural, political and the social. No wonder through critical questioning, Seers (1969) placed growth within a framework of larger social objectives, thus:

> The questions to ask about a country's development are therefore: What has been happening to poverty? What has been happening to employment? What has been happening to inequality? If all three of these have declined from high levels, then beyond doubt this has been a period of development for the country concerned. If one or two of these central problems have been growing worse, especially if all three have, it would be strange to call the result "development", even if per capita income doubled (p.3-4).

This questioning, thus, signalled the shift away from the goal of growth prompting the Human Development Report (1996: 10), to describe economic growth as a means and human development as the end of development. More importantly, such conception of development as economic growth allows dictators or tyrant leaders to use violence and other forms of coercion that can make life of their people unbearable by taking away most of their production as savings and investment surpluses in the guise of increasing national commodity out (Mabogunje: Ibid). Easterlin's conception of development is also contrary to the reality on the ground in many spheres of life in Africa where economic growth does not necessarily translate to the betterment of life of all people. In Botswana, for example, the national economic growth as a result of revenues from diamond sales has not benefitted other groups of people in the country such as the Khoisan. The same applies to Mozambique, whose annual national economic growth is considered as the fastest in Africa, estimated at between 4 and 6 %, yet the majority remain poor and languish in abject poverty (Mawere & Rambe 2013). Such criticisms levelled against Easterlin's conception of development (as economic growth) reveal that there is more to development than it is to increase commodity output or economic growth in general if development is to make human life better while promoting sustainability.

While Easterlin sees development as economic growth, some scholars have equated development to modernisation. Modernisation is "the process of social change in which development is the *main* economic component" (Lerner 1968: 387). The development scholar, Chambers (2004), for example, understands development simply as good change. Thus for Chambers, we can only talk of development where there is a social change perceived as good or positive. A critical look at Chambers' definition, however, reveals that since development concerns itself with good change, the implication is that development is something good as far as human life is concerned: good change implies positive change for purposes of better life for everyone. This implication is drawn from Chambers' elaborations as someone who argues that for a good change to occur there is need for "pedagogy of the non-oppressed" as opposed to "pedagogy of the oppressed" (Freire 1970). Yet while development understood as such implies collective better life, what exactly constitutes *good change* remains ambiguous, therefore, unclear especially considering the heterogeneity of both economies of the periphery (the so-called developing countries) and the centre (the so-called developed countries). In fact development is not enough for the word to be equal with the phrase "good change." Chambers, thus, seems unaware that development depends on values and on alternative conceptions of good life such that what development entails remains subjective and highly contentious in intellectual discourses and in both theory and practice.

Although development has been viewed from the lenses of economic growth and modernisation after the Second World War, by the end of the 1960s, it became apparent that neither development as modernisation nor as economic growth yielded the expected positive conditions and standards of living of the majority of the people in the so-called developing countries. Instead, the relative standards and conditions of living of the majority vis-a-vis that of the elite in these countries worsened (Mabogunje 1980), with abject poverty and destitution intensifying even more than ever before. For this reason, development came to be understood generally as distributive justice – justice needed to reduce poverty levels among the masses. This conceptualisation of development as distributive justice led scholars such as Swanepoel (2011: 72), to conceive development as "the opposite of poverty" given that it should strive to address the poverty of masses by satisfying their basic needs. Thus, for Swanepoel, development levels the ground between the poor and the rich. Yet, although this definition contains useful insights and quite appealing especially to many people of the so-called developing world, it is ambiguous in that it is implicitly unclear on what it exactly mean by development besides assuming that where there is development there is no poverty. This definition therefore largely accounts for the form of poverty widely known as community (or mass) poverty in developing countries and ignores relative poverty and case poverty – individual/individual family poverty – which is a common phenomenon in affluent societies of the Global North. Besides, it assumes (as does perspectives of development such as modernisation) that development projects always benefit all members of society (including the poor) whereas development, for example, understood as modernisation and industrialisation, tend to benefit the elite group and promote dependency syndrome between "developed" and "developing" worlds. This means that while it is true that development has the potency to address poverty and improve people's lives, it is not always the case that it does so in a manner that "avoids a situation in capitalist societies where the standard of living of the people could be poor in the midst of plenty" (Mawere 2014: 14). Instead, "real" development should level the ground between the poor and the rich by satisfying both their quantitative and qualitative livelihoods rather than widening the gap between the two or even worsen the lives of the masses. Besides, development should be futuristic. This is what is depicted in the quotation cited in the introduction of this chapter where I argue that development is not all about building roads, schools, hospitals and towns, but what we qualitatively do with the roads, the schools, the hospitals and the towns we build. In the quotation, I add a very important proposition that development is not only about the quantities of what is built, but what people benefit from all that is built for them and others to come. What people benefit from the process of development is critical. No wonder international development (also known as global development), the basis on which countries are classified as developed, developing or least developed, has faced intense criticism over the years. It is because it has tended to enrich some while impoverishing others such that it would be safe to argue that the so-called international development is a loop-sided deal meant to rig the world economy in the interest of the rich Global North by perpetuating the asymmetrical development-related relationships extant between the Global South and the Global North. In view of the visibly asymmetrical relationships between the North and the South in relation to the so-called international trade, I raise a number of critical observations and questions which trouble the concept of development further: Based on human basic needs, what is the component, criterion and true meaning of development? Should the meaning of development that the Northerners hold be always the same as that the Southerners embrace despite their different contextual cultural geographies? Why in the rating of development by the Northerners, though fall under material wealth, untapped resources such as minerals, wildlife, lakes, rivers, and forests are excluded in rating countries' levels of development? Isn't it baffling that even nonmaterial assets such as cultural richness are excluded in development rating of countries? In fact, isn't it that even we all have the idea that development should "positively" change and drive human needs towards the intent, what development really entails remain relative? With all these observations and questions, there is no doubt that there is more to what most developmentalists of the North say than they reveal, all to ensure that the North remains a victor. I argue here that in such a deal where lopsided victory prevails, it will be an abuse of the term "development" to subscribe it to this whole process of change. This is why I have already argued that "real" development should level the ground for everyone in society for it to pass the logic and reasoning of development proper. Putting that aside, let us hear more from other theorists of development on how they have conceptualised "development" and with what results.

Todaro (1992) as with Swanepoel, considers development broadly yet takes it as a multidimensional process that involves changes in attitudes, institutions, structures as well as acceleration of economic growth, the eradication of poverty and reduction of inequality among members of the society. In other words, Todaro sees development as a multidimensional process aimed at improving people's lives. For him, development should embrace three core values: firstly, the satisfaction of basic physiological needs; secondly, self-esteem; thirdly, freedom from man's servitude to nature, ignorance, other men, misery, institutions and dogmatic beliefs (see Todaro 1992: 100-102). As Musingafi *et al* (2013: 25) spell out, such development entails the following core values: "life sustenance, that is, the ability to provide for basic needs; self-esteem, that is the ability promote a sense of worth and self-respect and; freedom from servitude, that is, the ability to make choices which will influence or determine one's future." Thus, Musingafi *et al* are apt to argue that development should be holistic to the extent that it addresses people's freedoms, dignity, spiritual, and material concerns. In other words, Todaro as with Musingafi *et al*, are of the view development should have the utility to quench both quantitative and qualitative livelihoods.

This holistic understanding of development is not unique to Todaro and Musingafi *et al*. Other renowned scholars such Rodney (1972), the author of the legendary text: *How Europe underdeveloped Africa*, conceives development as increased capacity, skill, freedom, creativity, self-discipline, responsibility and material wellbeing. As Rodney was responding to the historical economic exploitations and inequalities that were created by Europe against the people of Africa, he argues for economic systems that liberate the whole person economically, culturally, morally, politically, and psychologically; hence his conception of development as a progress change in quantitative and qualitative terms.

The Tanzanian statesman-cum-scholar, Julius Nyerere also looked at development in almost a similar way, but from a people-centred perspective. Nyerere (1968) sees "development" as the development of people – human development in both quantitative and qualitative terms. He is against those who reduce development to quantitative betterment as for him, development is also about ascertaining qualitative livelihoods and human satisfaction. Nyerere, thus, argues that infrastructure such as buildings, roads and health facilities, among others, are not development in the strictest sense but only tools of development: they are means to achieve development and not the end of development. Basing on this understanding, Nyerere conceives development as a process in human society that fosters the general quality of human life and the natural environment in its totality. This means that Nyerere perceives infrastructures such as buildings and roads as tools of development because they help to promote quality human life as long as they don't upset the "natural balance," that is, as long as they do not impact negatively on the natural environment. For scholars like Sen (1999), such quality human life can be promoted by ensuring human freedom. Sen, in fact, sees freedom (and not development per se) as the ultimate goal of economic life as well as most efficient means of realising general welfare of all humanity. This connotes that for Sen, overcoming deprivation is central to development. In Sen's perception, human *unfreedoms* that society need to overcome include: hunger, famine, ignorance, an unsustainable economic life, unemployment, barriers to economic fulfilment by women or minority communities, premature death, violation of political freedom and basic liberty, threats to the environment, and little access to health, sanitation, or clean water.

In more or the same way as Sen and Nyerere, Peet and Hartwick (2009:1) have come to understand development thus:

> as making a better life for everyone. In the present context of a highly uneven world, a better life for most people means, essentially, meeting basic needs: sufficient food to maintain good health; a safe, health place in which to live; affordable services available to everyone; and being treated with dignity and respect. Beyond meeting these needs, basic to human survival, the course taken by development is subject to the material and cultural visions of different societies.

In this regard, the duo argues that development is change process aimed at improving human life through elimination of poverty. For Peet and Hartwick, the elimination of poverty is apparent among the people concerned when there are improved provisions of basic needs such as sufficient food to maintain good healthy, descent shelter to live in, clothing, and when the people are treated with respect and dignity.

Nevertheless, while it is true to a larger extent that whatever definition and interpretation of the term, development is about making life better for all people, there is a sense in which development understood as such could be considered as incomplete. This line of thinking is corroborated by the humanists, Wetmore and Theron (1998) who argue that development should encompass sustainable relations between the natural, environmental and the social. In view of their humanist approach to development, the duo further argue that since people are normative beings who create their own social reality such as norms and values, development cannot occur without the full participation of both experts and local actors as they are the ones who directly interact with the natural environment. In other words, Wetmore and Theron are of the view that development is only development as long as it promotes sustainability between the natural, environmental and the social, hence sustainable development. The Wold Commission Environment Report of 1987 conceives sustainable development as "development that meets the needs of the present without compromising the ability of future generations to meet their own needs" (Kendie and Martens 2008: 6). To summarise the duo's position, Wetmore and Theron (1998: 33) conclude that "development is not about the delivery of goods and services to a passive citizenry. It is about active involvement and growing empowerment." This means that development is not a one-way process but a dialectical one that should promote diversity and sustainability for it to be holistic – quantitative and qualitative – and long living.

Musingafi *et al* (2013: 34) concur with Wetmore and Theron that "development is not a one-off thing, but a process that has to be sustained." They underline that for development to be a community asset and sustainable, the people concerned should both participate and be empowered. Empowerment (also known as capacity building) is a process which open doors of opportunities previously closed to enable one to develop the ability to do things which were not previously within her competence (FitzGerald *et al* 1997). Such empowerment provides all people with the means to sustainably foster and manage development in their respective communities. This development founded on participation and empowerment – capacity building – is holistic, resilient and long living as it allows the acquisition of knowledge and skills, make productive resources available, and the establishment of effective and efficient administrative and institutional structures possible (see Swanepoel in de Beer and Swanepoel 2000).

Thus, while in the 1950s and 1960s, the focus of development was chiefly economic, this shifted in the 1970s, with the new focus of development casted to encompass economic growth and gross domestic product (GDP) as well as 'basic needs' (Streeten, Burki, Ul Haq, Hicks, & Stewart 1981). Development was now expected to satisfy human basic needs which included education, nutrition, health, sanitation and employment for the poor (Seers 1969; Harris 2000). This shift of development from economic to basic needs approach was now characterised by relatively less concern with economic indicators such as per capita income and national growth, but emphasised the quality of human life as well conservation of the natural environment. As argued by Harris (2000: 3), this shift in approach to development stimulated "the creation of the United Nations Development Programme's Human Development Index, which uses health and education measures together with Gross Domestic Product (GDP)" to determine development that guarantees human welfare in all societies. As Ghai (1977) explains, this new concept of human welfare is also concerned with 'redistribution with growth' (distribution of benefits/wealth of development among individuals, groups and regions) and became popular after the Cocoyoc Declaration in Mexico. The Cocoyoc Declaration puts it clear and loud that:

> Our first concern is to redefine the whole purpose of development. This should not be to develop things but to develop man. Man has basic needs – food, shelter, clothing, health and education. Any process of growth that does not lead to their fulfilment or even worse, – disrupts them is a travesty of the idea of development (Ghai 1977: 6).

The Declaration, thus, redefines development as a process of change that should be concerned with satisfying humans needs. It is this realisation for the need to cater for human needs that scholars like Seers (1969) argue that a country cannot claim to be developed when factors such as poverty, unemployment, and inequality are worsening, even if its per capita income doubles or triples.

Historical trends of development

The concept of "development" is not new in literature, though as a body of knowledge, it is relatively new. Its trends are distinctively three. The first trend dates from after the Second World War, particularly from the 1950s and early 1960s, when development discourse was dominated by modernisation theory. The second trend then stretches from the late 1960s to early 1970s, when development was dominated by dependency theory. The last trend ranges from the 1980s to the present period, where development is dominated by people-centred development perspectives. However, in literature, the concept of development dates back to the 19th century where it has been used in several fields in the areas of natural sciences, physical sciences and social sciences (cf. Abercrombie, Hill & Turner 1994; Cliché 2005). In the natural sciences, for example, the concept of development was used by Aristotle the philosopher to explain the nature of all things that develop as expounded in his theory of ladder of things. Other scholars like Charles Darwin used the concept in his theory of evolution of species where he explained that all species evolve over time, passing [or developing] from one stage to another (Cliche 2005).

Yet, while the concept of development has been so pervasive in the fields of natural sciences and the physical sciences, in the field of social sciences, development as a body of knowledge only emerged during the 1950s and 1960s following the end of the Second World War (Moll 1986; Treurnicht 1997; Harris 2000; Hettne, 2002). At this time, there was preoccupation by those in the social sciences on what should be done to help those societies that were badly affected by the war and those that were emerging from colonialism. Since this period, the concept of development has been associated with many disciplines such as social development, human development, sustainable development, political development, and economic development (Todaro 2000; Seers 1969; UNDP 1990; Adams 2006; Sen, 1999). It is in light of this that the concept of 'development' has become a multi-dimensional phenomenon which has been hotly debated globally throughout its history, conceptualisation and usage (Thomas 2004; Todaro 2000). For the same reason, some scholars have described development as an 'unstable concept' being both an urgent global challenge and a vibrant theoretical field for achieving an ideal future or a destructive myth (Edelman & Haugerud 2005). Others have conceived development as a 'contextual concept' or 'binary concept' focusing on Western cultures in relation to other cultures (Rist 1997; Hettne 2002).

As highlighted above, development, both as a process of change and an academic discipline in the social sciences began to obtain a more precise meaning for Western social scientists after the World War II. In fact, after the second world war, the major concern and issue affecting many societies of the world especially those conceived as "the underdeveloped countries" or "the developing countries" was the possible political and economic pathways these countries would possibly take as they were coming out of colonial rule, initially in the 1940s in Asia and, from the mid-1950s in several countries of Africa.

At this time, many social scientists, theorists, economists and organisations aimed at responding to a growing understanding of the complexity of development, thereby coming up with a variety of approaches as possible solutions and answers to the problem of underdevelopment of the time. Three major theoretical trends have since developed with modernisation theory being the first one stretching from the 1950s to the early 1960s. This was followed by dependency theory which stretched from the late 1960s to the early 1970s, before it was overtaken by the people-centred theory from the 1980s to date. It should also be noted that the post-World War II literature on economic development has been largely dominated by four major but sometimes competing approaches namely: the linear-stage-of-growth model such as that of Rostow, theories of development, patterns of structural change as those advocated by Marxism, and the free-market counterrevolution. I will focus on these post-World War 11 literatures in the next chapter. For now, it suffice to say that the prevalent supposition in the 1950s and 1960s was that 'Third World' countries would almost inevitably become developed over time unless they follow the path that the so-called 'Developed World' went through. In fact, the traditional wisdom of the time had it that sooner or later all countries designated as 'Third World' (or developing) would inevitably shift from a traditional to a modern state through two major drivers namely, economic and technological advancement. This was in spite of the fact that there was a subsequent emergence of many new countries, mainly in Africa and Asia, joining the existing long-independent, yet still mostly "underdeveloped" countries in different parts of the world.

Conclusion

To sum up this chapter, it should be noted that what is understood as "development" in contemporary discourses is a matter of contention to the extent that some scholars such as Dudley Seers (1977: 3) has wondered if "instead of worrying about brushing aside the web of fantasy and slipshoddiness surrounding the word 'development,' we shouldn't simply abolish its use and look for a better and less debased word". Nevertheless, it should be underscored that while the definitions and interpretations conjured throughout history and those elaborated above differ in diction and vantage points, they hold a shared recognition to the extent that they generally agree that ultimately development should be a holistic and progressive process of change concerned with the improvement of the general quality of human: it should progressively and positively transform the lives of both men and women as well as their society to a more habitable one. In fact, a critical look at "development" reveals that although it is multi-faceted with no distinct direction and has enjoyed varied interpretations, it is clear that whatever development entails, its ultimate goal should be improved quality of life of both the people and the natural environment. Thus, real development should improve collective lives by ascertaining both qualitative and quantitative livelihoods that do not upset the natural balance – the relationship between animals (including people) and plants.

Chapter 2

Development and Underdevelopment in Africa: Through the Lens of Theory

"Theory has so far proved to be a double sword. It is a double sword that cuts from both ends. While liberating, theory also oppresses as it has done to Africa's development jam. Through foreign theories that African leaders have unwittingly allowed to sprawl obtusely, today, Africa remains locked in the grips of underdevelopment" (Munyaradzi Mawere 2016).

Introduction

As is noted in my proposition above, theory, particularly foreign-made theories, have done inconceivable harm to Africa's development. It is largely through the deployment of Northern-fabricated theories that today Africa remains poor, poorer than she was at the eve of independence in the 1960s. It is through such theories that African leaders, in the name of promoting international development, unwittingly and unintelligently have allowed the Westerners to experiment on their economies using the prescriptions of neoliberalism of the International Monetary Fund (IMF) and the World Bank, framed policies of Structural Adjustment Programmes (SAPs), which in no doubt have witnessed the cataclysmic fall of the African economies and ensured dependence on Western corporations and countries. With these Western-bred policies, which were flaunted as bringing development and salvation to African economies when in fact they served as the vanguard of imperialism, one can hardly singles out any economy on the continent whose sanity was spared in the face of these suspicious remedies. This makes critical African minds even doubtful if *Development Studies* as an academic discipline exported from the North and the modules incorporated therein were indeed meant to instil and foster development in Africa. Given the failures of the SAPs and many Western theories of development to move the wheels of African development, one is tempted to argue that even the discipline of *Development Studies* itself as exported from the North, particularly its content, should be treated with caution, lest it is meant to divert the attention of Africa from the real, true and objective issues that matter for the continent. In fact, while academies across the continent have recently embraced the disciplines and modules on development, I warn that the notion of *Development Studies* much like that of civilisation that culminated into African colonialism, should be critically scrutinised, especially its content, before it is offered in the African academies. This would afford the African academies with the opportunity to approach the discipline from a contextual point of view and prevent African students from drinking toxic theories and models of development that will either intoxicate or subject them to eternal intellectual fatalism. In fact, I challenge African academies to make sure that the *Development Studies* programmes and other such disciplines and modules on poverty studies, as they are largely exported from the Global North, are structured to address the specificities and realities of the African people and the continent at large both at theoretical and practical levels. I say this because from my postgraduate studies of *Development Studies* at university, I realised that most of the content seldom address, not even mention, Africa's primary causes of poverty and underdevelopment such as the continued looting of African resources, the West's denial to pay reparations or compensate Africa for its cardinal sin of colonialism, the denial of the West to return some of the looted invaluables such as artefacts and gold pieces, epistemicide, robbing, exploitation, and enslavement. In classes, I often raised the question why such issues are nowhere in the modules meticulously addressed when we are in fact studying development in order to initiate and foster development on the continent and beyond? In fact, isn't it that we should have comprehensive modules focusing on why and how Africa was looted, robbed, plundered, and exploited by Western corporations and capitalists given that these constitute the major problems and challenges for the continent at least both historically and practically? By avoiding such modules in our academies, isn't it that we are celebrating irrelevance at the expense of that which can help us as a society? It seems it is for the same reason that African scholars like Nyamnjoh (2012a,b) has argued that many African academies and scholars have excelled at intellectual irrelevance on the continent often by acting as zombies and clearing agents for Western discourses [in this case, by including those modules that privilege development and poverty discourses from a Western perspective while excluding burning concerns on matters of pillaging/looting, plundering, restitutions and compensation] that hijack African popular agendas. Thus, isn't it that we should have space where we discuss comprehensively when and how inequality in Africa started? Sadly, I never got any satisfactory answer tempting me to think that development discourse as exported from the West is meant to divert the attention of Africans and all the formerly colonised states from reclaiming what was looted, robbed, exploited and disinherited from them in the false name of civilisation. Thus, one wonders if development in so far as it is currently deployed does not constitute Western hypnotic efforts to neutralise African struggles for ownership and control of their resources. By the same token, I have been prompted to take the bull by its horns and audaciously assume the task of theorising development in Africa.

As highlighted in chapter one of this book, the environmental, political, and socio-economic situations in the so-called Developing World societies (also known as Third World countries) such as Africa have been an issue of concern most especially since the Second World War through contemporary times. The question that has remained boggling for many critical minds has been: "How come Africa is so underdeveloped whilst it is one of the richest continents on earth?" What could be the force behind this puzzle? Is it because Africa is super rich and its people too beautiful for "predators" to leave the continent and its people alone? One could possible think so given that everything that is beautiful in the eyes of many is vulnerable, and in turn, anything that is vulnerable is easy to fall prey to predators. Yet this has ever been the thinking of the theorists during and after the Second World War. In response to the development issues and problems of Third World societies, a large body of theory from theorists of development has emerged. This includes integration theories and disengagement theories of development. These theories have, however, met with criticism. That being the case, this chapter seeks to examine the assertion whether both integration and disengagement theories of development have failed Africa in as far as development in and on the continent is concerned. Using a historical hermeneutical approach, integration theories will be critically examined before disengagement theories of development are reflected upon. While acknowledging the importance of the aforementioned theories in stimulating the development debate and generating insights on issues and problems associated with development, the chapter argues that both integration and disengagement theories of development have, among many other factors, failed Africa development-wise.

Theories of development

As highlighted above, there are many theories of development, that is, theories that were believed to instil and propel development in Third World countries (also known as least developed countries), produced by the so-called Global North and exported to the Global South. These were:

a). Integration theory

Integration theories of development (that are closely linked to modernisation theories) have approached and conceived development through the lens of economic growth. In view of this approach, the foremost and proponent scholar of integration theories, Walt Rostow views development in the developing world through the lenses of economic evolution. Being the most influential and outspoken advocate of the linear-stages theory, Rostow, among other prominent scholars, believed that the rest of the world needed to look up to the Western model of development (rooted in modernity) and copy and adapt to the Western trend of development in order to make progress. In his infamous book, *The stages of economic growth: A non-communist manifesto*, Rostow (1960), argues that if they are to develop, developing countries (such as those of Africa) should pass through a number of stages of economic growth that are similar to those which have been experienced by Western Europe. For Rostow, these stages were: the traditional society, the preconditions for take-off/change (transitional stage), take-off, the drive to maturity, and the age of high mass consumption.

Rostow's five stages of economic development
i). Traditional society

According to Rostow, all societies commence their development process as traditional societies. At this stage, such societies will be characterised by:

- Low agricultural productivity;
- Crude technology;
- No savings;
- High birth rates;
- Insistence on traditions;
- Resistance to change;
- High proportion of the labour force in the agriculture sector;
- Low capital;
- High illiteracy rates;
- Hierarchical social system;
- Kin-orientedness and,
- Production for subsistence.

ii). Preconditions for take-off

The second stage for any society, according to Rostow, is preconditions for take-off. At this stage, the society concerned will have made some considerable progress towards economic growth.

This will be possible on the pretext that the society have now managed to overcome the prejudices and limitations of tradition, which characterise the first stage of development in any society. The preconditions are however not internally induced, but induced from the outside in the forms of invasions, colonialism and imperialism, among other forces. Above all, these preconditions should be induced from the Global North. The referred forces – colonialism, invasions or imperialism – take over and dominate the traditional elements of the traditional society to hasten the undoing of tradition and to initiate a complete change in the traditional society. Thus, societies at preconditions stage are characterised by the following:

- New belief in private profit as opposed to the spirit of communalism and collectivism;
- Rise in entrepreneurship;
- Centralised governance of both the economy and politics;
- Capital accumulation;
- Population control;
- Training of labour force/human resource development;
- Investment in infrastructure;
- Employment oriented strategies;
- Expansion of the education sector and;
- Emergency of new political and economic elite that prioritise the modernisation of the economy.

iii). Take-off

This stage, for Rostow, is characterised chiefly by rapid growth of the economy. This economic growth is instilled by investment in and the spreading of Western technology in both the industrial and agricultural sectors of the society's economy. Without the diffusion of technological changes in both the agricultural and industrial sectors, the society, thus, cannot take-off, but remain stagnant. This stage, thus, is characterised by two main tenets namely;

- The emergence of political, social and institutional set-ups that are conducive for a steady growth of the economy;

- The emergence of rapidly agricultural and industrial sectors;
- More integration into the capitalist system through removal of factor prices biases and through capital accumulation as well as liberalisation of the economy.

iv). Drive to maturity

Once the society demonstrates that it now has technological skills which it can be able to sustain over time, it is moving towards maturity. At this stage, the society can produce whatever it chooses to produce simply because it has all the technology and know-how to do so. This stage is characterised by:
- High technological skills;
- Entrepreneurial skills and;
- Liberalisation of the economy.

v). Age of high mass consumption

According to Rostow, this is the final stage of development for any society in the world. This level of development is reached when a society is now in a position to cope with the consumption patterns and lifestyles of its people. This stage is normally characterised by:
- Social security and welfare programmes for vulnerable groups such as children, the aged and women;
- Rise in personal income such that consumption of societal members are no longer limited to the basics or necessities.
- The economy shifts towards durable consumer goods;
- Self-sustaining economy;
- More efficiency;
- High transparency level in the society.

Thus, for Rostow, the above explicated stages are the stages at which all societies should pass through if they are to be as developed as the Western societies. As Rostow (1960: 1-3) himself wrote in the opening chapter of his *Stages of Economic Growth*:

This book presents an economic historian's way of generalising the sweep of modern history [...]. It is possible to identify all societies, in their economic dimensions, as lying within one of five categories: the traditional society, the pre-conditions for take-off into self-sustaining growth, the take-off, the drive to maturity, and the age of high mass consumption [...]. These stages are not merely descriptive. They are not merely a way of generalising certain factual observations about the sequence of development of modern societies. They have an inner logic and continuity [...]. They constitute, in the end, both a theory about economic growth and a more general, if still highly partial, theory about modern history as a whole.

As could be seen from his assertion above, Rostow's understanding is that the industrialised countries of the Global North had all gone beyond the stage of "take-off into self-sustaining growth," while the underdeveloped countries that were still in either the traditional society or the "preconditions" stage had only to follow a particular series of tenets of development to take-off in their turn into self-sustaining economic growth.

A critical analysis of the assertion above, however, reveals that Rostow reasoned as if development was evolutionary and linear in nature, that is, as if development passes through clearly defined stages. He failed to note that development is multi-dimensional and in fact do not assume any direction as it should move (at least "positively") all areas linked to it. More so, Rostow failed to note that Western economies grew largely because they retained ownership of their resources, pillaged (or looted) and plundered the resources of others (such as Africans) in the world. Also, Rostow did not realise that Western economies developed not because they invested in economic goods but simply because they had enslaved others through forced labour. For these reasons, Rostow's theory of development has been criticised for being too simplistic and unrealistic as it assumes that development is a natural process that occurs linearly. More importantly, Rostow's approach, as that of integration theories in general, has been accused of failing the economies of the so-called developing countries especially in Africa where his theory has been exported as an ideal model of development. In fact, a close look at Rostow's theory vis-a-vis Africa reveals that since colonialism through postcolonial period, Rostow's ideas have been imposed on the African countries in one way or another through the philosophy of one-size-fits-all; a philosophy which assumes that conditions and circumstances of all people around the world are the same regardless of their different situations and contexts. By using the philosophy of one-size-fits-all, Rostow's theory has failed to pay due attention on the context and circumstantial factors associated with development. In many African countries, for example, the institution of Economic Structural Adjustment Programmes (ESAP), which just like colonialism, could be understood to have been exported and instituted in Africa in view of Rostow's pre-condition for take-off stage, have in no doubt had cataclysmic effects on many economies on the continent. In Zimbabwe, for example, with the introduction of ESAP, the standard of living of the general populace fell drastically as the programme culminated in loss of jobs, high levels of unemployment, and increased cost of basic commodities. No wonder in his Conference speech, de Castro (1968) argue that "one of the greatest mistakes *by developmentalists* was to consider that the process of development everywhere should be equal to the model of the rich Western countries," which also justify that integration theories of development have failed Africa as far as development is concerned.

I should underline that Rostow's conception of development falls within the framework of the macro-theory of modernisation perspective of development, particularly the integration theory. This perspective sees development as a process that is only catching up with the Western world (MacPherson 1982). In fact, the modernisation perspective is a socio-economic perspective that recognises the positive role played by the developed countries in facilitating development in developing countries. It perceives "the present and past developing countries' situation as an original state of development, which is the stage of traditional society through which the now advanced capitalist countries had also passed" (Musingafi *et al* 2013: 28). In this sense, development in Africa as in other developing countries of the world, is viewed in evolutionary terms as moving directly from traditional society through several stages (as those enunciated by Rostow) up until a stage when it is at par with development in the Global North, particularly North America and Western Europe. It is arguably true that, it is from this understanding that in the 19th century, colonialism was inveigled and instituted in Africa in the false name of civilisation while some amounts of foreign aid (through international financial institutions such as the World Bank and the International Monetary Fund) and the provision of external technical assistance were rendered to Africa on the pretext that development would "catch up" with Africa as it did with Western Europe. Yet, critical analysis of the effects of colonialism on Africa reveals that colonialism marginalised the African "other" and impoverished Africa while enriching the Western world in ways too numerous to mention (see Rodney 1972; James 1954; Mawere 2014a, b; Mawere and Mubaya 2016). Rodney (1972), for example, argues that through colonialism and other such forms of exploitation, Europe looted African resources – both material and human capital – to develop its own empire. On the same note, some scholars have argued that foreign aid (through hand-outs and technical assistance) rendered to Africa in the name of development by the non-governmental organisations from the Global North is meant to keep check on African socio-economic growth while perpetuating and ensuring the cultivation of dependency syndrome and undermining development on the continent (Mawere 2014a). This is true when one looks at African countries such as Mozambique, Zambia, Malawi and many others, which now largely depend on donor funding to sustain their economies. In addition to this criticism, Mabogunje (1980:27) has accused integration theories of development for "overlooking the global expansion of metropolitan capital, ignoring its inner dynamics during the imperialist stage and paying little attention to its impact on the space economy of peripheral societies found in underdeveloped countries." It is from these lines of thinking and reasoning that one can argue that integration theories of development such as the modernisation perspective have failed Africa in as far as development in and on the continent is concerned.

b). Modernisation theory

Modernisation theory, which was largely written and developed within the framework of North America's experience, emerged in the 1930s with the early development initiatives of colonialists and economists, but gained momentum in the mid-twentieth century (the 1950s), to be applied to many other societies of the world. In fact, in the 1950s, theorists particularly economists and sociologists from the Global North, began to theorise about how development in newly independent countries and those countries badly affected by the Second World War could initiated. The modernisation theory appeared from an American orientation after the Second World War for three major political reasons. First, the United States emerged as the single powerful hegemony of the world. Second, the Soviet Union vigorously defended *development* through socialism and it made clear that it wanted to spread and lead socialism around the world. Third, new countries in Latin America and Africa were emerging as independent after decades of colonial rule (So 1990: 17). Modernisation theory was in fact deemed as a political and economic tool for the United States to justify her intervention in any nation that sought any path contrary to the interests of capitalism (Escobar 1997). This theory investigated the modernisation of nation-states and argued that economic development promoted political development: it underlined that economic development is a prerequisite for political development. Yet, economic development was only possible if and only if the traditional society relegates to the periphery all its traditions and adopts those of the Global North, particularly of the so-called Developed World. This means that for modernisation theory, economic development and political development were inevitably compatible. Put differently, at the heart of the modernisation theory is the underlying assumption that the structures and processes of all human societies in the world develop from simple forms of traditionalism to complex modern societies.

On this basis, it was, therefore, argued that many developing countries such as those of Africa's poor political systems were a result of their economic underdevelopment. In the 1950s, modernisation theory, gained credibility with many scholars such as Walt Rostow, Western governments and international financial institutions. As such, modernisation theorists of the 1950s and early 1960s mistakenly regarded the process of [economic] development as a series of successive stages of economic growth through which all countries of the world must pass if they are ever to be developed (see for example, Rostow's stages of development). These theorists, thus, principally believed that, following modernisation theory, what the Third World only required to allow was a progression along an economic growth pathway that has been traditionally followed by the Developed World. And, for them, this was only possible with the appropriate amount and combination of saving, investment, technological diffusion and foreign aid from the Global North. This prompted many scholars of the time to think that development is synonymous with rapid, aggregate economic growth and nothing more nothing less.

Arguing from a modernisation perspective of development, Goran Hyden (1980; 1983), for example, developed an economy of affection approach to explain underdevelopment in sub-Saharan Africa and how a breakthrough could be achieved in Africa's matrix of development. With his approach, Hyden argues that the peasant mode of production (and kinship ties) – what he called economy of affection – common in sub-Saharan Africa defies capitalism and modern development. Thus for Hyden, Africa's underdevelopment is not a result of international capitalism as instigated by the West and the Americas. Rather, such underdevelopment results from the resilience of pre-capitalist and pre-modern structures of Africa's countryside where the kind of personal relationships and dependencies form the basis for subsistence economy – what Hyden himself call "economy of affection". As Hyden thinks, this resilience do not only resists economic progress but kills the spirit of development as a whole because it stifles values of capitalistic market.

For Hyden, such anti-development is even compounded by the fact that peasant mode of production as that of Africa operates according to the law of nature as opposed to the law of value. This, as Hyden envisages, gives rise to the economy of affection and leaves out the peasants yet to be captured.

Yet, just like Rostow's theory of development and the mainstream modernisation perspective of development itself, Hyden's approach to development has been accused of failing Africa development-wise. The pejorative labelling of traditional structures and indigenous technologies of Africa as pre-modern and pre-capitalistic, for example, could be argued to have had tremendous effects on Africa's development. It has led to the loathing of and failure to include African indigenous technologies in the education and development agenda of Africa, thereby betraying development on the continent. A case in point is the dissuasion of Africans by Westerners to rely on "traditional medicines" by caricaturing all practices of healing by Africans as "Black magic" and witchcraft. Put differently, with the sneering of African indigenous modes of production as pre-modern, Africa was denied the opportunity to exploit its own readily available resources to instil development and determine her own destiny as a continent, hence the argument that integration theories of development such as Hyden approach have failed Africa in as far as development in and on the continent is concerned.

Besides, modernisation theorists such as Rostow, Hyden, Huntington and Almond idealised the economic state of the United States and Europe as the model that all "underdeveloped countries" should be follow if ever they are to develop; thus outlining any aspect of the cultures of the so-called "underdeveloped nations" as undesirable if they do not correspond to the Western concept of modernity.

More so, the main focus of modernisation theory is utterly on the internal conditions of the countries, thus leaving the external factors behind, in addition to the profound colonial heritage most developing nations still hold (So 1990: 54). It is on the bases of such reasoning that integration theories of development were accused of failing Africa and other such erstwhile colonies' development, disengagement theories were developed as an alternative to fostering and promulgating Africa's development. In fact, basing on the failures and weaknesses of the integration approaches and strategies of development, the disengagement theories call for a total disengagement of the "developing world" with the world capitalist system. Proponent theorists in this school of thought, thus, "believe that there has been too much integration through colonialism and neo-colonialism" (Musingafi *et al* 2013: 31), and it is this integration that failed or "underdeveloped" Africa while furthering development in the Global North.

Thus as could be seen, both the modernisation and integration theories have fallen short as far as African development is concerned. Yet, the biggest error that Africans have made in the history of development is to assume that Northern models and theories of development are inherently perfect, just, fair, objective, ethical and moral when the reality is that they are grossly imperfect, unfair, immoral, unjust, and exploitative.

c). Globalisation theory

Related to the modernisation theory discussed above is the "globalisation theory." Globalisation theory is a theory of development (Reyes 2001) that uses a global mechanism of greater integration with particular emphasis on the sphere of economic transactions. It is a United States of America and Europe-centric positive model of development whose main thrust is to spread features of capitalism around the globe. The focus of globalisation theory is communications and international ties, with these ties directed at cultural and economic factors in communication systems.

The globalisation theory explains poverty and inequality by identifying cultural and economic factors in global connection. In explicating the theory of globalisation, Reyes (2001: 2) claims there are two major meanings of the word "globalisation". One deals with the word as an event when a sense of interdependence occurs throughout different countries of the world in different aspects of communication, trade, and finance. The other meaning that has been applied to the concept of globalisation considers it as a theory of economic development with the supposition of widespread unification among different countries. This integration is believed to have an effective influence on the development of economies and on the improvement in social indicator. The question that remains unanswered even today is whether globalisation really contributes to the socio-economic development of economies of developing countries.

For Zineldin (2002), unlike the thinking displayed by pro-globalisation theorists, one can witness the problems that have been produced by globalisation in developing countries. He, like other scholars such as Akandele (2002) and Aborishade (2002), traces the origin of such globalisation related problems to developing countries competing rather than cooperating with each other. Zineldin, however, focuses more on religion other than culture as Aborishade and Akandele do. Religion, (Zineldin 2002) argues, can affect globalisation in exactly the same way that culture can, as demonstrated by the instruction in the Quran that cooperation is based on piety and goodness and shuns malice and devilish deeds (Qur'an, verse 2 in sura 5; Zineldin 2002: 39). Zineldin (2002: 39) takes Arabic countries, as examples of places where, according to Islam, such an idea will help the sense of cooperation needed in implementing globalisation theory. Similarly, Hamid and Craig (1993) generalised the notion of religious cooperation to include not only Muslim but also non-Muslim countries across the world.

d). Disengagement theory

One of the scholars of disengagement theories, Frank (1967) argues that the survival of 'traditional" institution and capital shortage are not responsible for underdevelopment in the developing countries (also known as the Third World). For him, underdevelopment in the developing countries such as the majority of those in Latin America (as those in Africa) is a result of the same historical process which generated the development of capitalism. Josue de Castro (1970) corroborates this view when he argues that underdevelopment is not lack of or insufficient development but a product or sub-product of development as underdevelopment derives inevitably from the colonial and neo-colonial economic forms of exploitation which continue to unfairly impose themselves on many regions of the world. Vincent (1995) aptly captures this line of thinking when he avers:

It is capitalism which has produced the imbalances in the world which are at the root of poverty, and hence the political tensions which we experience. It is therefore patently obvious that this system is inadequate, since it has been deeply tainted through the appropriation of wealth, capital, the means of production, and revenue by a small minority (p. 6).

On the basis of this understanding and his experiences of continuing underdevelopment in Latin America, Frank as with Vincent and de Castro, came to believe that the unequal and exploitative relationship between the centre (imperial economies of the Global North) and the periphery (developing economies of the Global South) rebuts the liberal assumption central to the integration theories that underdevelopment in developing countries is a result of insufficient understanding and use of Western technology, frameworks, models and policies. Frank, instead, argues that underdevelopment in the developing countries is chiefly a result of asymmetrical and exploitative relationships the imperial powers of the Global North and their clientele of the Global South. Connelly *et al* (2000), agree with Frank and Vincent to the extent that they understand the causes of underdevelopment in the developing countries to be emanating from:

i. Persistent outflow of economic surplus;

ii. Historical positioning of developing countries in the international economy;

iii. The exploitation and use of the present-day underdeveloped and developing countries as sources of cheap raw materials, markets for their goods, and outlets for surplus capital by the now industrially developed economies; and

iv. The fact that present-day developing countries cannot expect to pass through the same stages of economic development that the now industrially developed economies went through.

What Connelly *et al*, as with Frank, Vincent and de Castro argue in essence is that, there is need for the developing countries such as those in Africa to disengage themselves totally from their previous unequal economic relationships with the imperial powers of the Global North if they are to develop themselves while becoming self-sustaining.

However, a critical analysis of disengagement theories shows that it is equally flawed such that the theories have also been criticised for failing Africa in as far as development in and on the continent is concerned. Musingafi *et al* (2013: 32, emphasis original), for instance, argue that though sound and to some extent convincing, "it is not practical that a country, *especially from a developing world* disengages itself completely from the world systems in the current global village." They give an example of Zimbabwe who after disengaging herself from the Commonwealth and other such international institutions critical to her policies resulted in chaos, disintegration, and the 2007/2008 economic crisis. It is from such real examples, that one can argue that disengagement theories, just like integration theories, have failed Africa in as far as development in and on the continent is concerned.

To further their argument, Musingafi *et al* (Ibid), articulately note that the other way disengagement theories have failed Africa development-wise is its fiasco to "clearly spell out what needs to be done after disengagement in a step-by-step format," which however would have been charged of prescription and inflexibility context-wise. By failing to provide an exit way or path for disengaging countries, disengagement theories are tantamount to leaving developing countries in the cold and with no exit strategies, thereby failing their economies. It is from such reasons that one can argue that disengagement theories have failed Africa in as far as development is concerned.

Theories of underdevelopment

Just like theories of development, theories of underdevelopment were also given by development scholars of the first generation. Besides, most of these theories were similarly postulated by development theorists from the Global North, with not even a single theory from within Africa. These theories, though exported from outside, were meant to account for the reasons why Africa was underdeveloped and indeed remained as such. Some of these theories include:

a). Dependency theory

About two decades after the postulation of the modernisation theory, modernisation theorists started having a torrid time explaining the rising disparities within Third World countries and for growing international inequity. In fact, a very small number of countries were achieving anything resemble what scholars like Rostow, for example, termed "take-off" stage. Worse still, for those few that resembled Rostow's characterisation, growth was often uneven and inconsistent. This realised frustrated the Third World countries, which thought they were being fooled by the Developed World to waste time trying to implement measures that are never helpful in resuscitating their economies.

The talk on dependency theory is said to have originated with two papers published by two scholars in 1949, one by Hans Singer and another by Raul Prebisch – Singer-Prebisch thesis –, in which the authors observed that resources flow from a "periphery" of poor and underdeveloped states to a "core" of wealthy states, enriching the latter at the expense of the former. In fact, the central thesis of dependency theory is that poor states are poor simply because they have been (and continue to be) impoverished by the rich states through the way these poor states are integrated into the "world system." This theory arose as a reaction to modernisation theory, an earlier development theory, which held that all societies progress through similar stages of development as those that the Developed World went through such that the task of the Developed World has the task to accelerate development in Third World by various means such as technology transfer, investment and closer integration into the world market. Dependency theory, thus, totally rejected the modernistic view arguing that underdeveloped countries have unique features, contexts and structures of their own and most importantly are poor because of their asymmetrical and exploitative relationships with developed countries. Dependency theory which rose from 1950s onwards mainly from the research of the Economic Commission for Latin America and the Caribbean (ECLAC) with prominent representatives such as Prebisch, thus viewed underdevelopment in Africa, Asia, and Latin America as a product of development of the Western countries. The major points of the Prebisch model are that in order for development in a country to occur, it is necessary to:

i). Control the monetary exchange rate by placing more governmental emphasis on fiscal rather monetary policy;

ii). Promote a more effective and responsible government in terms of national development;

iii). Create a platform of investments by giving a preferential role to national capitals;

iv). Allow the entrance of external capital in line with priorities already established in national plans for development;

v). Promote a more effective internal demand in terms of domestic markets as a base to reinforce the industrialisation process

vi). Generate a larger internal demand by increasing the wages and salaries of workers, which will in turn positively affect aggregate demand in internal markets;

vii). Develop a more effective coverage of social services from the government, especially to impoverished sectors in order to create conditions of competitiveness;

viii). Develop national strategies according to the model of import substitution by protecting national production and establish quotas and tariffs on external markets (Bodenheimer 1970: 49-53).

Prebisch's model acted as a basis for dependency theory especially in the earlier days, other dependency theorists such as Baran (1973), Frank (1971, 1972), Furtando (1973) and Rodney (1972), strongly argued that the less developed countries of Africa, Asia and Latin America should be fully comprehended as the periphery of the developed countries (centre). Frank, for example, advanced the argument that the underdevelopment of the periphery is an inevitable reflection of the development of the core. In short, for dependency, the so-called "underdeveloped" have been conditioned to become culturally, economically/materially, politically, and psychologically dependent on the so-called the developed world.

Another eloquent proponent of dependency theory is Andre Gunder Frank. Frank, using predominantly historical experiences of Latin America, sought to investigate the problem of underdevelopment in the so-called Third World countries. From his findings, Frank established that the causes of the underdeveloped status of Third World countries (such as those of Latin America and indeed Africa) today are closely linked with the historical causes of development in the currently industrialised and developed nations of the world. More specifically, Frank fundamentally argued that development and underdevelopment are deemed as two features of the same system: they are an obverse of one system. Furthermore, Frank argues that the industrialised and developed countries of world were never underdeveloped at any given moment, but they were in fact at some time in history undeveloped. Frank argued as because, in his view, underdevelopment is not a historical stage of growth through which industrialised (and now developed countries) countries proceeded, but instead, it is the consequence of the historical development of the capitalist system. What has made the Third World countries to remain underdeveloped, further argues Frank, is their contacts with the industrialised (and now developed countries) countries through colonialism which was indeed exploitative economically. To add more value to his argument, Frank further outlined a number of hypotheses regarding his central argument on development and underdevelopment of the nations of the world. His first hypothesis highlighted the world embracing asymmetrical metropolis-satellite structure with which he advanced that as a result of such metropolis-satellite relationship (or what I call here centre-periphery relationship), the metropolis (countries of the global north) tend to develop while the satellites (countries of the global south) tend to underdevelop. His second hypothesis claimed that the satellites can only encounter their greatest economic development if and when their links to their metropolis are weakest. Frank reasoned, thus, because he believed that the relationship between the metropolis and the satellite was asymmetrical and exploitative of the satellite nation-states. Frank's third hypothesis was that those regions that are perceived as the most underdeveloped nowadays are the ones that had the strongest bonds to the metropolis at one time in history. This strong link of the currently underdeveloped to the metropolis resulted in excessive exploitation of the former thereby culminating in their underdevelopment. Frank's fourth hypothesis was that "the greater the wealth that was available for exploitation in the past, the poorer and more underdeveloped the region today; and the poorer the region was as a colony, the richer and more developed it is today" (Frank 1975: 97-98). Frank's main points of his central thesis and hypothesis are summarised in Table 1 below:

It should be underlined that for dependency theorists, the problem of underdevelopment in the underdeveloped regions (such as Africa) is seen as an external phenomenon such that for them it is over and over again development itself that in fact triggers it. As Sunkel and Paz (in Seligson 1993: 205) put it:

> Both underdevelopment and development are aspects of the same phenomenon, both are historically simultaneous, both are linked functionally and, therefore, interact and condition each other mutually. This result […] in the division of the world between industrial, advanced or "central" countries, and underdeveloped, backward or "peripheral" countries […].

Table 1: Frank's Micro-Macro Structures of Underdevelopment and Development

Micro-Structure of Development/Underdevelopment	Macro-Structure of Development/Underdevelopment
Relates to the structure of a backward country having periphery (p) and metropolis (m).	Relates to the structure of Capitalist world having its peripheries (P) and metropolis (M). The peripheries are nothing but the metropolis of so many backward countries.
A backward state centre (m) is a periphery of world capitalism.	Metropolis of world capitalism is not a periphery of anybody or anything.
Within the micro-system of a country, surplus is extracted from (p) and sent to (m)	Within the macro-structure of capitalist world, surplus is extracted from all dependent colonies/state centres (m), and it goes to the metropolis (M).
Trough loss of surplus, (op) becomes underdeveloped, and (m) becomes comparatively developed when surplus is extracted from state metropolis (m) by the world metropolis (M), (m) becomes underdeveloped. Thus, both (p) and (m) become underdeveloped through macro-structural exploitation.	No surplus is lost, but it is gained from all dependent colonies/states. Hence, (M) becomes developed. There is no mechanism/agent to extract the surplus of macro-metropolitan centre (M).
Macro capitalist structure unfavourably influences the micro-structure of a backward country and produces underdevelopment in LDCs.	No exploitation is possible by the micro-structure. Macro-centre (M) develops uninterruptedly. Micro-structure of LDCs helps the development of the macro-structure in industrialised countries.

Source: Gosh, B. N. 2001. *Dependency Theory Revisited*, Burlington, Vermont: Ashgate Publishing, pp. 50-51.

Thus, underdevelopment theorists generally view the centre [developed countries] as competent of vigorous development receptive to internal needs which makes it the chief beneficiary of the global relations. On the other hand, the periphery [developing countries] is viewed as having an impulsive type of development, which is both restrained by its integration into the global system and its adjustment to the conditions of the expansion of the centre. It is this condition that dos Santos (1970: 180) explains when he argues that:

> Dependency is a situation in which a certain number of countries have their economy conditioned by the development and expansion of another […] placing the dependent countries in a backward position exploited by the dominant countries.

From the theories of development (such as modernisation) and underdevelopment (such as dependency), one can note that they compare and contrast in many ways. In Table 2 below, I compare and contrast the modernisation paradigm with the dependency paradigm as a way of throwing more light on how theorists from both ends conceptualised the nature and causes of development and underdevelopment in different areas of the world.

b). Spatio theory

For other scholars such as Landes (1998) geography and climatic conditions of some regions of the world (such as Africa) were responsible for the underdevelopment of Africa. Landes, thus, refused to accept that dependency was solely responsible for the underdevelopment of regions such as sub-Saharan Africa. For him, climate and geography are important factors for economic growth and societal development as people normally avoid the extremes in climate and geography. On this note, Landes argued that there are a couple of key differences in hot and cold climate. First of all, if you are settled in a cold climate you can find shelter against the cold, build a fire for getting heat or cover yourself in furs and wool. In hot climate there is no real solution other than air conditioners and they are expensive and relatively new inventions. Second, biologically speaking, there is a difference between one who lives in cold weather and that living in hot weather. When humans use their muscles, for

Table 2: The Modernisation and Dependency Paradigms

	Modernisation Paradigm		Dependency Paradigm	
	Early Theorists	Later Theorists	Dependency Theory	World Systems Theory
Causes of Underdevelopment	Nations start out underdeveloped. Lack of modern technology, capital, entrepreneurial spirit, modernising elites.	Vicious circle of poverty. Internal colonialism Lack of social differentiation and social mobilisation	Capitalist exploitation Unequal terms of trade Comprador elites Lack of spin-off effects of primary export production	Historical emergence of capitalist world system since 16th century creates international division of labour, within which each country has its function
Structure of the System	Internationally: developed and underdeveloped countries Internally: traditional and modern sectors	Internationally: developed and underdeveloped countries Internally: dual traditional and modern economies "Colonial" dominance by a major	Developed centre and underdeveloped periphery	Developed core, underdeveloped periphery, partially developed semiperiphery

		city or region		
Path to development	Underdeveloped countries must follow the paths traversed by developed countries	Foreign aid and foreign investment to overcome vicious circle of poverty Open trade Export production – at first of primary resources, then of manufactured goods	Import substitution to develop the domestic economy Acceptance of foreign investment but with strong controls to break dependency	May be necessary to "delink" from the capitalist world system for a time Countries can move from periphery to semiperiphery to core
Key Theorist(s)	Walt Rostow	S.N. Eisendstadt	Andre Gunder Frank	Immanuel Wallerstein

Source: Ted C. Lewellen. 1995. *Dependency and Development: An Introduction to the Third World,* Westport, Connecticut: Bergin & Gravey, pp. 68.

example for work, they generate heat. In cold climate this is not unpleasant since they can get rid of this heat if needed, yet in hot and wet climate (as those of Africa), this is not the case. This lowers productivity. The hot climate is unpleasant and has made people "invent" things like siesta to use the day in the best possible way, argues Landes. Third, Landes argues that the climate of tropical regions such as those of Africa have the side effect of being a very good environment for parasites and diseases. This is especially true in sub-Saharan Africa, where a cleansing frost like the one that the temperate climates gets, is not present. The rain cycles of sub-Saharan Africa are much more varied, irregular and heavier than in Northwestern Europe. Hence, for Landes (1998), Africa's underdevelopment is a result of its own geography and climatic conditions.

c). World systems theory

World system is the inter-regional and transnational division of labour, which divides the world into core countries, semi-periphery countries and periphery countries (Barfield 1997). By core countries we mean those countries of the developed world with capital-intensive production, high skill and technology, and semi-periphery countries are those countries that have relatively capital-intensive production and skill, while periphery countries refers to those countries with low capital-intensive production and skill as well as low levels of technological advancement. For dependency scholars such as Frank and Rodney, it is from the periphery countries where the core extracts raw materials and markets its finished products to enrich its industries and continue dominating the semi-periphery and periphery countries.

It should be noted that as a system, world system is dynamic as it keeps on changing with time. This is because individual countries can either gain or lose their core to regress to the semi-periphery or even to the periphery (Wallerstein 1974). Wallerstein gives an example in the last few centuries, when the world system has extended geographically and intensified economically with the core status passing from the Netherlands to the United Kingdom and most recently to the United States of America.

In the 1970s, Wallerstein produced what is believed to be the best known version of world-systems analysis where he traces the rise of capitalism in Europe. From his analysis of capitalist world-economy, Wallerstein concluded that the rise of capitalism was an accidental outcome of the protracted crisis of feudalism. Western Europe used its advantages and gained control over the development and spread of industrialisation and capitalist economy indirectly resulting in unequal development. Yet, Wallerstein argued that core countries do not exploit poor countries a dependency theory argues. He gives two reasons why this is true: First, core capitalists exploit workers in all zones (the core, the semi-periphery and the periphery) and not only workers from the periphery countries. Second, core countries do not exploit periphery states as dependency theory proposes because capitalism is organised around and inter-regional and transnational division of labour. For Wallerstein, there is instead division of labour between the core countries and the semi-periphery and periphery countries.

d). Slave trade theory

While the three theories of underdevelopment explained above are the ones commonly found in literature, I add two more theories which I believe help to explain underdevelopment in Africa at both theoretical and practical levels. These theories are slave trade theory and beauty theory. I start by explaining slave trade theory.

Thus, related to world systems theory is what I call the "slave trade theory". With this theory, I explain, through the lens of theory, how slave trade underdeveloped Africa. Slaves were legally defined as property (Wax 1973) and slave trade itself understood as a form of business. As Moreno Fraginals (1977: 1900 writes "the slave trade was the business that involved the greatest amount of capital investment in the world during the eighteenth and nineteenth centuries. For proponents of this theory, Africa's underdevelopment today can be explained in terms of the history of extraction and exploitation as characterised by slave trade and subsequently colonialism, which did not only impoverish the African continent at the time but whose effects continue to be felt even today some decades after its "legitimation." For them, given that Africa's slave trades were an important factor affecting both political and economic underdevelopment, they may be a central reason behind Africa's weak states and economies today. At a world scale, four distinct waves of slave trade were experienced between 1400 and 1900, and during the different periods: 1400-1599, 1600-1699, 1700-1799, 1800-1900. Nathan Nunn (2007: 3-4) captures this aptly when he records that:

> Between 1400 and 1900, the African continent experienced four simultaneous slave trades. The largest and most well-known is the trans-Atlantic slave trade where, beginning in the 15th century, slaves were shipped from West Africa, West Central Africa and Eastern Africa to the European colonies in the New World. The three other slave trades – the trans-Saharan, Red Sea, and Indian Ocean slave trades – are much older and predate the trans- Atlantic slave trade. During the trans-Saharan slave trade, slaves were taken from south of the Saharan desert to Northern Africa. In the Red Sea slave trade, slaves were taken from inland of the Red Sea and shipped to the Middle East and India. In the Indian Ocean slave trade, slaves were taken from Eastern Africa and shipped either to the Middle East and India or to plantation islands in the Indian Ocean.

Of the four waves of slave trade enunciated above, trans-Atlantic slave is worth noting, not because the other waves were insignificant but mainly because of the large numbers of people that were shipped from Africa to Europe. As Nunn (Ibid: 4) further tells us "during the trans-Atlantic slave trade alone, approximately 12 million slaves were exported from Africa. Another 6 million were exported in the other three slave trades. These figures do not include those who were killed during the raids or those who died on their journey to the coast". It should be further noted that Africa's slave trades were also distinctive in that unlike previous slave trades, individuals of the same ethnicities enslaved one another as a result of hatred, witchcraft accusations, and greediness. This had serious detrimental effects on Africa's socio-economic and political development as it caused social and ethnic fragmentation, political instability, weakening of states, and the spreading of corruption.

While it can be argued by some scholars that slave trade has ended, overwhelming evidence continue to show which demonstrate that slave trade in Africa and many other parts of the world such as Asia continue even today, besides the negative effects it has always had. But how did trans-Atlantic slave affected (and indeed continue to affect) development in Africa?, one may ask.

In view of the question above, it can be argued that slave trade in Africa had more than economic effects to the continent of Africa. First and foremost, slave trade created a sense and environment of uncertainty, internal conflict and insecurity to the people at the time, the kind of insecurity that continues even today. During the time, individuals required weapons such as spears, arrows, iron knives, swords or firearms, to defend themselves. Most of these weapons could be obtained from Europeans in exchange for slaves. Due to uncertainties created by the first wave of slave trade, many people especially local chiefs and individuals of repute found it worth participating in slave trade to guarantee their security. Most of the slaves were often obtained through local kidnappings and "gun-slave" by either Europeans agents or Europeans themselves. The sense of insecurity created by the first wave of slave trade, thus, perpetuated slave trade and amplified the degree of insecurity among the African population. This ultimately resulted in a vicious cycle where some would enslave others to protect oneself (Mahadi 1992; Hawthorne 1999). It can be argued that it is this vicious cycle that prompted community raidings in southern Africa such as those by Tshaka of the Zulu, the Kololo and the Ndebele people of Zimbabwe. In western Africa, as far as 1526, Affonso, King of Kongo (today Democratic Republic of Congo), wrote to Portugal complaining of the Portuguese traders of the time that "there are many traders in all corners of the country. They bring ruin to the country. Every day people are enslaved and kidnapped, even nobles, even members of the king's own family" (Vansina 1966: 52). In central Africa and many other parts of western Africa, well-documented examples come from the Balanta of modern day Guinea-Bissau, the Minyanka of modern day Mali (Klein 2001), and the Makua, Chikunda, and Yao of East Central Africa (Isaacman 1989; Alpers 1969). Hawthorne (1999; 2003) provides detailed studies in Cassanga of modern day Guinea Bissau where to protect themselves and their communities from being raided, [traditional] leaders often chose to pay slaves as tribute to the European traders, which against the traditional norm were often obtained through the judicial systems of the [traditional] chiefs. As Hawthorne further reveals, the Cassanga chief used the 'red water ordeal' to procure slaves for European traders as well as to procure possessions from his subjects, but all in the name of the judiciary system. Those accused of a crime were forced to drink a red concoction. If they vomited, then they were judged to be guilty. If they did not vomit, they were deemed not guilty. However, the concoction has a double effect as for those that did not vomit this ultimately brought death by poisoning while those deemed guilty had their possessions seized and their family members sold into slavery. In eastern Africa, particularly in the late 19th century, slave trades are well-known for having disintegrated the once intact Shambaa kingdom, Gweno kingdom, and Pare states in the Pangani Valley (see for example, Kimambo 1989; Mbajedwe 2000). In short, slave trade sowed the seed internal conflict and political unrest, which obstructed the complex state system formation in the continent of Africa. These conflicts, insecurities, uncertainties and political unrest have, unfortunately, continued compromising peace and stability even today in many African countries with succession conflicts (whether chieftainship or presidential succession) being a talk of the day, yet their roots could be traced to grudges and alien *cultures* of the slave trade.

Also, slave trade, just like colonialism, was a form of corruption meant to enrich some while impoverishes others. As Manning (1990: 124) argues "slavery was corruption: it involved theft, bribery, and exercise of brute force as well as ruses. Slavery thus may be seen as one source of pre-colonial origins for modern corruption." Bairoch (1993: 8) echoes the same sentiments when he argues that "there is no doubt that a large number of negative structural features of the process of economic underdevelopment have historical roots going back to European colonisation". Given the number of human capital in the form of slaves, besides material resources in the form of raw materials, that were shipped from Africa to Europe, there is no doubt that "Europe underdeveloped Africa" (Rodney 1972). It is well documented that during the trans-Atlantic slave trade, slaves were taken in their greatest numbers from the 'Slave Coast' (now Benin and Nigeria), West Central Africa (Zaire, Congo, and Angola), Ethiopia, Sudan, and the 'Gold Coast' (now Ghana). Other African countries like South Africa, Gabon, Namibia, Zimbabwe, Zambia, among others, exported relatively low numbers of slaves (see also Manning 1983). Below is a table showing the number of slaves per country that were shipped from Africa to Europe.

Table 3
Estimated total slave exports between 1400 and 1900 by country

Isocode	Country name	Trans-Atlantic	Indian Ocean	Trans-Saharan	Red Sea	All Slave Trades
AGO	Angola	3,607,020	0	0	0	3,607,020
NGA	Nigeria	1,406,728	0	555,796	59,337	2,021,859
GHA	Ghana	1,614,793	0	0	0	1,614,793
ETH	Ethiopia	0	200	813,899	633,357	1,447,455
SDN	Sudan	615	174	408,261	454,913	863,962
MLI	Mali	331,748	0	509,950	0	841,697
ZAR	Dem Rep of Congo	759,468	7,047	0	0	766,515
MOZ	Mozambique	382,378	243,484	0	0	625,862
TZA	Tanzania	10,834	523,992	0	0	534,826
TCD	Chad	823	0	409,368	118,673	528,862
BEN	Benin	456,583	0	0	0	456,583
SEN	Senegal	278,195	0	98,731	0	376,926
GIN	Guinea	350,149	0	0	0	350,149
TGO	Togo	289,634	0	0	0	289,634
GNB	Guinea-	180,752	0	0	0	180,752

	Bissau				
BFA	Burkina Faso	167,201	0	0	0	167,201
MRT	Mauritania	417	0	164,017	0	164,434
MWI	Malawi	88,061	37,370	0	0	125,431
MDG	Madagascar	36,349	88,927	0	0	125,275
COG	Congo	94,663	0	0	0	94,663
KEN	Kenya	303	12,306	60,351	13,490	86,448
SLE	Sierra Leone	69,607	0	0	0	69,607
CMR	Cameroon	66,719	0	0	0	66,719
DZA	Algeria	0	0	61,835	0	61,835
CIV	Ivory Coast	52,646	0	0	0	52,646
SOM	Somalia	0	229	26,194	5,855	32,277
ZMB	Zambia	6,552	21,406	0	0	27,958
GAB	Gabon	27,403	0	0	0	27,403
GMB	Gambia	16,039	0	5,693	0	21,731
NER	Niger	133	0	0	19,779	19,912
LBY	Libya	0	0	8,848	0	8,848
LBR	Liberia	6,790	0	0	0	6,790
UGA	Uganda	900	3,654	0	0	4,554
ZAF	South Africa	1,944	87	0	0	2,031
CAF	Cen African Republic	2,010	0	0	0	2,010
EGY	Egypt	0	0	1,492	0	1,492
ZWE	Zimbabwe	554	536	0	0	1,089
NAM	Namibia	191	0	0	0	191
BDI	Burundi	0	87	0	0	87
GNQ	Equatorial Guinea	11	0	0	0	11
DJI	Djibouti	0	5	0	0	5
BWA	Botswana	0	0	0	0	0
CPV	Cape Verde Islands	0	0	0	0	0

COM	Comoros	0	0	0	0	0
LSO	Lesotho	0	0	0	0	0
MUS	Mauritius	0	0	0	0	0
MAR	Morocco	0	0	0	0	0
RWA	Rwanda	0	0	0	0	0
STP	Sao Tome & Principe	0	0	0	0	0
SWZ	Swaziland	0	0	0	0	0
SYC	Seychelles	0	0	0	0	0
TUN	Tunisia	0	0	0	0	0

Source: *Nunn 2007: 13*

It can be argued that there is omission of data for countries in Southern Africa – namely Swaziland, Botswana, and Lesotho – and many other countries that may have suffered slave trade. It is almost impossible, for example Swaziland and Botswana not to have suffered slave trade at all considering their adjacency to the sea. This is because adjacency to the sea was one of the important determinant factors for slave trading as sea routes were usually to transport slaves to Europe. Yet, as could be seen in table 1 above, it is indubitable that through slave trade Africa was deprived of its human capital, besides other problems that came along with the trade.

e). Beauty theory

Elsewhere (Mawere 2016), I have noted with reference to Africa that beauty is dangerous! It makes one vulnerable, and since everything that is vulnerable is easy prey to predators, so is beauty. I add that just like sweet sugar, beauty attracts all. It is common knowledge that where there is sugar, ants come in thousands. So is where there is beauty. Predators come from all walks of life to prey on the beauty. Now, why am I talking of beauty with reference to the continent of Africa? My answer is very simple, but complicated in a way! After pondering for a long time about why Africa is so underdeveloped when in fact it is one of the richest continents in the world in terms of natural resources, I found part of the answer to this puzzle in Africa's beauty which like sugar attracts all kinds of ants. I found out that Africa is full of rich reserves of beautiful and precious natural resources ranging from minerals to plants, from wild animals to plenty of sunshine, and from abundant tracts of land to beautiful beaches. Human capital of quality and strength cannot be left out on the list; the major reason why Europe was so attracted to the people of Africa during slave trade. Now how the beauty of Africa has made it vulnerable and an easy prey to predators?

With all the aforementioned unique and beautiful resources that exist in abundance in Africa, the continent has attracted so much the eyes of the predator. The "predator", from afar, has for a long time set an eye of admiration and envy on Africa. Being attracted to the beauty of Africa, the predator has put in place all mechanisms and structures to prey on Africa's beautiful resources – both natural and human. These mechanisms range from the historic slave trade to capitalism, colonialism and neo-colonialism, the latter of which is currently in full force. Through these nefarious mechanisms, the predator has plundered the rich resources of Africa and thwarted the rights of Africans as a people, rendering them a voiceless people worth nothing but exploitation by others.

It is obvious that natural beauty hardly erodes! So, has been the beauty of Africa. Africa's beauty has continued shining lustrously for centuries now, stretching from the 1400s when slavery was set to prey on the sons and daughters of Africa. Since that time, the predator has always been preying on the beauty of Africa. The resilience of Africa's beauty has witnessed despicable atrocities and travails of the African people perpetrated by the envious predators in different episodes – slave trade, capitalism, colonialism and neo-colonialism; episodes that have all sowed the seed of underdevelopment on the African soil. Thus, the underdevelopment of Africa, though attributable to other possible causes, is largely a result of the continent's resilient beauty that like sweet sugar has always attracted predators of all kinds to prey on the continent's beauty.

Africa on the path of development

Having demonstrated that both integration theories of development and disengagement theories have failed Africa in as far as development is concerned, one then wonders what Africa should do to permanently eradicate poverty and achieve the highest level of development possible or at least to achieve development comparable with that of the Global North. After noting weaknesses and failures associated with both the integration theories and disengagement theories, Vincent (1995) suggests that the solution to promote development and eradicate poverty in developing economies such as those of Africa can have its source in paradigm shift from the rigid capitalist mentality to "a social and solidarity-based economy, centred around individuals and on satisfying their needs, and which will lead not only to the sharing of the means of production and of income, but also to the sharing of decision-making power" (p. 7). One can agree with Vincent's social and solidarity-based economy paradigm shift, most importantly because, as Vincent spells it himself, the paradigm entails:

i. Redistribution of wealth and the means of production;
ii. Worldwide justice and solidarity;
iii. Full employment for everyone;
iv. Access to power, knowledge and know-how, for everyone; and
v. Freedom of expression and of organisation for everyone.

It is indeed clear that such a paradigm shift is people-centred such that if allowed, it has the potential *not* to upset the natural balance and to influence changes in structures, institutions and attitudes which promote *sustainable* development and symmetrical relations between different stakeholders in society.

Besides, the paradigm shift has the potential to allow generative dialogue between different socio-economic and environmental epistemologies, be they approaches, paradigms and models. It has the potential, for example, to promote sustainable development that allow a generative balance of nature as well as the fusion and complementary working together of Western and African oriented development strategies, which are likely to promote collective development that make life better and desirable for all people.

Conclusion

In conclusion, it can be argued that while theoretical prescriptions such as the integration theories and the disengagement theories are important to historically and hermeneutically understand the nature of socio-economic situation and prevailing circumstances in Africa, they have both failed to provide solutions for Africa's development problems such that more soul searching in the area of development studies is more urgent now than ever. Instead, people-centred approaches seem to be more plausible and likely to promote *even* and sustainable development anchored on social justice, economic growth, and equality as has been demonstrated in this chapter and indeed in this whole book.

Chapter 3

The Blame Game and Politics of Development in Africa

> *"The cause of underdevelopment in Africa is a problem that if it is to be singled out will remain ever elusive and tantalising for as long as it has ceased to exist in solitary but entangled in matrices of politics and blame games. It is a problem that now requires only a multidisciplinary scientist to disentangle"* (Munyaradzi Mawere 2016).

Introduction

It has already been underlined in the preceding chapters that the question on the causes of underdevelopment in the so-called Developing World societies (also known as Third World countries) has been an issue of concern especially since the Second World War through contemporary times. It has been worrying why some societies seem to be more developed than others and vice versa. The question though has gained tremendous prominence in intellectual discourse over the years in both Africa and beyond, it however, remains peculiarly difficult to respond in a word and with precision. This is chiefly because, when it comes to development discourse on Africa, on one hand, there is a group of people who believe that Africa's underdevelopment is a plight of its own making and, on the other hand, there is a group of those who argue that Africa's underdevelopment is externally engineered and therefore never a plight of its own making. One remains wondering what really is behind Africa's underdevelopment predicament. Or even before asking that: What underdevelopment really entails?

Owing to the nebulous nature coupled with the contested possible causes of underdevelopment, a robust comprehension of the term "underdevelopment" and analysis of its causes as a troubling phenomenon, calls into question its practical manifestations and applications in particular situated contexts such as those of the Third World countries of Africa. It remains pertinent to understand whether underdevelopment only exists in the so-called Third World countries, while development only resides in the so-called Developed World countries. It also remain apposite to understand who defines development and underdevelopment and for whom. More still it remains appropriate to question the scale used to measure development and likewise that of underdevelopment. Whose scale is it? How does it measure development and underdevelopment in a world where materiality mingles fluidly with immateriality?

In view of this background and questions raised, this chapter seeks to unpack what underdevelopment is and is not in view of various theoretical lenses of development and scholarly researches over the years. The chapter further interrogates the notion by some scholars that Africa's underdevelopment is a plight of its own making. In this attempt the chapter unpacks the ambiguities and controversies associated with the alleged causes of underdevelopment in Africa.

What underdevelopment is?

The concept of "underdevelopment" as that of development itself has been notoriously understood by scholars such that no one definition is universally accepted. For example, in economics in general, underdevelopment is a situation that obtains when resources are not used to their full socio-economic potential, with the result that local or regional development is slower in most cases than it should be (Frank 2005). Yet, Frank is quick to highlight that underdevelopment also results from the complex interplay of internal and external factors that allow less developed countries only a lop-sided development progression. As spelt out by FAO (1948), symptoms of underdevelopment include lack of access to job opportunities, health care, drinkable water, nutritious adequate food, education and housing and also "a wide disparity between the rich and poor populations, and an unhealthy balance of trade" (Frank 2005: 32). This realisation of underdevelopment as multi-dimensional made scholars like Josue de Castro (1968a) to argue that underdevelopment is not lack of development per se, but a product or sub-product of development that results from an ill-guided kind of universal development or misuse of natural and human resources.

As could be seen, the different interpretations of underdevelopment proffered throughout history are largely dependent on the orientations of the authors. In this book, underdevelopment shall be understood as a situation that obtains when a nation-state lags behind most others in industrialisation, education, standard of living, healthcare, utilisation of natural resources (unutilisation or under-utilisation), life expectancy and other technological and cultural norms such that access to the basic necessities [needs and wants] is limited and life lived by the majority is "undesirable." By undesirable life, I mean life that no average person would wish or desire to live. It is also emphasised that underdevelopment implies that a country has potentials and possibilities to develop as the resources are therein available but either underutilised or unutilised (see also Viner n.d: 2).

Causes of underdevelopment in Third World countries

What exactly cause[d] underdevelopment in the so-called underdeveloped countries remains complex, eluding and indeed difficult to unpack and pin down with precision. Many factors are said to have prevented underdeveloped nations such as those of Africa from developing naturally such that most of these countries remain trapped in the bracket of poor nations or the so-called underdeveloped countries. As underlined above, the causes of underdevelopment especially in view of Africa have been highly contested such that there are no universally agreed answers to the question of causes. On one hand some scholars have argued that Africa's socio-economic and political underdevelopment is externally induced while on the other hand it has been argued that Africa's underdevelopment is self-caused – a plight of its [Africa] own making. Some of the alleged causes of underdevelopment in Africa are as follow:

Trans-Atlantic slave trade, colonialism and neo-colonialism

Those who subscribe to the theory of externally induced underdevelopment like many African statesmen, scholars and theoreticians draw their arguments from the general notion that Africa's underdevelopment is a result of past imperial and exploitative experiences such as slave trade and colonialism by the Global North. Kenneth Grundy (1966), who did research with a number of statesmen of Africa, particularly from Ghana, Guinea and Mali, for example, noted that the statesmen openly attributed the underdevelopment of their respective countries to the direct result of European enslavement of Africa and colonialist exploitation of the African people and resources. For them, Europe's past (and indeed the present) exploitation of Africa played (and continue to play) a significant role in the underdevelopment of Africa. The statesmen, according to Grundy, further retort that before the advent of trans-Atlantic slave trade and European colonialism, Africa had vibrant promising socio-political and economic systems which were severely disrupted by the Europeans as they exploitatively create wealth for themselves. As Grundy assertively tells us:

In their view, colonial rule has prevented the socio-economic development of Africa in the interests of the indigenous masses. Quite accurately, they content that the Europeans regarded the African economy as an appendage of the metropolitan economy, to be exploited for enhancing the national power, profit and prestige. The Europeans took slaves, profits, and raw materials out of the continent [...] and left virtually nothing in return. The resulting conclusion is that, in order to foster development in their own interests, Africans must terminate colonial political control (p. 63).

In particular, Sekou Toure (1959: 39) of Guinea asserts that "imperialist domination brought about the fragmentation and destruction of the pre-colonial African economy." Toure (Ibid) further asserts that "the colonial system took our goods at a very paltry price and sold them at a very high price. The profits [...] did not go to the producers who were the real creators of the products, the true owners of the products; they went through many middlemen [...] into the cashboxes of the colonialists." As such, Grundy (1966) concurs with Toure that Africa's level of development is a product of the economic conditions brought about by foreign intervention and domination.

Toure and Grundy's argument resonates with Awolowo (1961: 3) who argues that:

> The scramble for Africa as well as the permanent settlement of Europeans in certain parts of Africa was motivated wholly and solely, and without any redeeming feature, by the political, economic and military self-interests of the European powers which engaged in that unholy adventure.

Toure and Grundy's argument also reverberate with Manning (1981), Inikori (1992), Gemery and Hogendon's (1979) argument that Africa's engagement in the trans-Atlantic slave trade culminated into its underdevelopment as this caused massive depopulation of the continent over two centuries. For the aforementioned scholars, this depopulation in turn resulted into an implosion of the continent's production possibility frontier and an unambiguous reduction in welfare, thereby plunging the continent into economic underdevelopment. Besides, the transfer of labour – human capital – from Africa to Europe in the form of slaves included a large percentage of skilled tradesmen and women from a range of occupations and professions who were making their contribution to African societies, thereby depriving Africa of socio-economic gains.

Similarly, the famous Guyanese Marxist historian and political activist, Walter Rodney ascribes the underdevelopment of Africa to the asymmetrical power relationships between Europe and Africa. In his masterpiece work, *How Europe underdeveloped Africa*, Rodney (1972: 137) argues that:

The decisiveness of the short period of colonialism and its negative consequences for Africa springs mainly from the fact that Africa lost power. Power is the ultimate determinant in human society, being basic to the relations within any group and between groups. It implies the ability to defend one's interests and if necessary to impose one's will by any means available. In relations between people, the question of power determines manoeuvrability and bargaining, the extent to which a people survive as a physical and cultural entity. When one society finds itself forced to relinquish power entirely to another society that in itself is a form of underdevelopment.

As Rodney noted, Africa was deliberately exploited and underdeveloped by Europe through a combination of asymmetrical power relations and economic exploitation. For Rodney, the asymmetrical power relations between Africa and Europe continue even today – through neo-colonialism. With this in mind, one can argue that the exploitation of Africa by Europe did not end with the demise of colonial administration in Africa (Mawere 2014a). In fact, the existence of the "invisible hand" or the towering ghost of colonialism on the African soil perpetuates underdevelopment on the continent (Mawere 2014b). This line of thinking is corroborated by scholars like Alcott (n.d) who argues that:

> Africa has never freed itself from domination by the West. In the late twentieth century and in the twenty-first century, the relationship between the West and Africa has been primarily one of exploitation. International trading agreements with Africa have been unfair on African countries. These agreements have been overly influenced by Western big businesses. Such unfair agreements and relationships have allowed individual African officials to get rich while the region sells itself cheaply and develops no infrastructure. This relationship of exploitation has been a common feature of the European intervention in Africa. It started with the arrival of the missionaries, and continued with

the arrival of European merchants and mercenaries, and most lately, with the Western multinational corporations.

Supporting the same line of thinking as that of Alcott and Rodney, among others, de Castro (1968a), in his speech delivered on the 4th of April 1968, had this to say:

> Third World countries are underdeveloped not because of natural reasons but mostly because of historical facts because of the power of circumstance. Unfavourable historic circumstances, especially political and economical colonialism, which kept these regions aside from the rapidly growing world economy.

In another speech at a Conference in 1970, de Castro's (1970) assertively noted that:

> Underdevelopment is not the lack of development. It is the result of an ill-guided kind of universal development. It is the abusive concentration of income, especially during this historic period dominated by capitalist neo-colonialism, which is responsible for much of the underdevelopment in the world today: the regions that are direct political or economical colonies.

As is clearly spelt out in de Castro's assertion above, underdevelopment is not necessarily an equivalent of poverty as it implies "the abusive concentration of income" especially in the so-called capitalist neo-colonialism, a period that others would want to call "supercolonialism". Supercolonialism because for them, colonialism has never ended to qualify as "neo-colonialism" but only continues in camouflaged sort of names.

Imposed foreign global economic policies
Besides colonialism and neo-colonialism, foreign global economic policies imposed on Africa by the Global North have also been charged for failing African economies. This has been coupled by the

continued existence of the Western-based corporations and institutions in Africa. In fact, much the same as in the larger part of the early colonial era when colonial corporations such as New Guinea Company, German South West Africa colonial Company, British South African Company, East India Company and Dutch East India Company were established and others chartered to govern territories on behalf of the Western monarchies and imperialists (Kitamura 1969; BBC, 17 February 2011a,b), the postcolonial scenario has done worse to retain foreign corporations and institutions of the former colonisers that are indebted to their home countries governments. And, it is in fact through companies that countries like German and France, for example, managed to retain their colonialism even after they had formally lost colonies in Namibia and West Africa respectively (BBC, 17 February 2011a, b). Kitamura's (1969) observation thus is apt when he reports that:

> With German colonialism, a series of companies were organised playing an important part in the activity of German imperialism. After World War I, notwithstanding loss of all the colonies, 85 companies were newly organised or reorganised and shouldered the task of continuing colonialism without colonies.

All this together with the institution of neoliberal polices by the International Monetary Fund and the World Bank impacted negatively on the African state of poverty, inequality and underdevelopment. Naiman and Watkins (1999) observe in view of the International Monetary Fund's (IMF) Enhanced Structural Adjustment Facility (ESAF) such as Economic Structural Adjustment Programme (ESAP) in sub-Saharan Africa that:

> Developing countries worldwide implementing ESAF programmes have experienced lower economic growth than those who have been outside of the programmes. African countries subject to ESAF programmes have fared even worse with their per capita incomes declining than other countries

pursuing ESAF programmes. It will be years before these populations recover the per capita incomes that they had prior to structural adjustment.

As Naiman and Watkins (Ibid) further observe, in sub-Saharan Africa, external debt rose from 58 % in 1988 to 70 % in 1996 as a result of the IMF's ESAF programmes. This has resulted in these developing countries diverting resources from expenditures on health care and education in order to service external debt. Besides, annual real per capita GDP growth averaged 0.0 % (from 4 % annual economic growth in the case of Zimbabwe) and 3 % decline in real per capita incomes for all ESAF countries over the period 1991 – 1995, whereas non-ESAF developing countries experienced, on average 1. 0 % annual real per capita GDP growth (IMF Internal Review 1997: 5). Again, in sub-Saharan Africa, countries that adopted ESAP were "forced," as a matter of policy, to reduce government spending, eliminate government subsidies, privatise government enterprises, and liberalise their economies. Whatever results all these economic policies yielded, it remains important to note that the policies were misguided by the modernisation theory of development which advanced that economic growth was a necessary condition for development of the so-called developing countries. Unfortunately, these policies saw more poverty and underdevelopment towering Africa than any other time before as many people lost their jobs and prices of commodities rose sharply beyond the buying power of the majority. Living experiences in Africa (as those in Latin America) show that the modernisation theories (through foreign aid and other capitalistic approaches) have failed dismally (cf. Chambua 1994). As Raftopoulos (1998) note, poverty remains a norm in Africa producing:

- Ruthless growth (growth associated with increasing inequality and poverty);
- Jobless growth (growth without expanding employment opportunities);

- Voiceless growth (growth without extending democracy or empowerment);
- Rootless growth (growth that withers cultural identity);
- Futureless growth (growth that squanders resources needed by future generations).

Thus, while growth, as anticipated by developmentalists from the Global North, is a necessary condition for human development, it is clear from Raftopoulos's analysis above that growth in itself is an insufficient condition for human development. The 1981 Zimbabwe World Bank Report corroborates this line of thinking when it reveals growth in Rhodesian economy that: "while economic growth taking place in the country allowed luxurious and privileged lifestyles to the small white community, black women and their families were forced to live out in a life of grinding poverty in the reserves" (p. 2). Colman and Nixson (1994) also confirm the same thinking when they argue in view of their observations in Latin America that Gross National Product (GNP) per capita may increase while at the same time inequality increases and the poor becoming poorer and negative progress being registered towards other development goals. The modernisation theory, which has been the dominant guide to the main aid organisations like USAID and the economic policies of the frontline international financial institutions such as the World Bank and International Monetary Fund (IMF) was, therefore, misguided to believe that economic growth is the necessary condition for human development in developing societies of the world. It is against this backdrop that one can argue that Africa's underdevelopment is externally induced and, therefore, not a plight of its own making.

Diseases

There are some scholars and theorists who think otherwise. For them, Africa's underdevelopment is internally induced such that it should be understood by unpacking the prevailing political and socio-economic dynamics within the continent itself. Bloom and Sachs (1998), Gallup and Sachs (2001), Batten and Martina (2005) and Bhattacharyya (2007), for example, ascribe underdevelopment in

Africa to diseases such as malaria and other infectious ones, with which they argue that they have fatal as well as debilitating effects on the human population in Africa. For these scholars, the diseases negatively and directly influence productivity, savings, and investment which ultimately affect economic performance of the continent as a whole. To single out one of these scholars, Bhattacharyya (Ibid) argues that:

> Malaria incidence [...] affects development by increasing both mortality and morbidity. Increased mortality resulting from malaria induces households to increase current consumption and save less for the future. Increased morbidity on the other hand adversely affects productivity. This slows down capital accumulation and economic growth (p. 3).

Bonnel (2000) supports Bhattacharyya when he argues that in 2000, the rate of growth of Africa's per capita GDP was reduced by 0.7 % per year from 1990 – 1997 with a further 0. 3 % per year lower in countries also affected by malaria. In view of HIV/AIDS, Bell *et al* (2003) also argue that HIV and AIDS have affected the economic growth of Africa by reducing the availability of human capital, thereby contributing to its underdevelopment. Using his research findings in Cote d'Ivoire, Over (1992) confirms that the sharp increase in adult mortality due to diseases in Africa has shifted the responsibility and blame from the family to the government in caring for orphans, which in turn is worsening the continent's underdevelopment.

Poor governance
For other scholars like Soren Jacobsen (2014), poor governance, lack of political will and corruption are the principal causes of underdevelopment in Africa. In his own words, "sub-Saharan Africa has massive problems with corruption and the political system is responsible for many of the problems that sub-Saharan Africa have because of political leaders that have found it more important to

enrich themselves and stay in power than develop their countries" (p. 3). Corroborating the same line of thought, de Castro (1968b) argues in a speech that:

> Underdevelopment is a product of misuse of natural and human resources which will forcibly deviates regions from economical expansion and avoid social changes needed to join human groups in an integrated economical system. Underdevelopment and hunger can only be eliminated from the face of the earth through a global development strategy which will mobilise production means in the interest of the community.

No wonder scholars like Landes (1998) argue that when the Europeans left Africa after the demise of colonial administration, the Africans were not yet ready to govern themselves as they lacked the capabilities. This, for Landes, explains why after colonialism in Africa, the political and economic situation on the continent even worsened with political unrest, ethnic wars, and inflation recorded at their highest.

Geography and climatic conditions

Besides political will, corruption and poor governance, Landes (Ibid) also cite geography and climatic conditions as the other factors responsible for the underdevelopment of Africa, especially sub-Saharan Africa. For him, climate and geography are important factors for economic growth and societal development as people normally avoid the extremes in climate and geography. He goes on to argue that there are a couple of key differences in hot and cold climate. First of all, if you are settled in a cold climate you can find shelter against the cold, build a fire for getting heat or cover yourself in furs and wool. In hot climate there is no real solution other than air conditioners and they are expensive and relatively new inventions. Second, biologically speaking, there is a difference between one who lives in cold weather and that living in hot weather. When humans use their muscles, for example for work, they generate heat. In cold climate this is not unpleasant since they can get rid of this heat if needed, yet in hot and wet climate (as those of Africa), this is not the case. This lowers productivity. The hot climate is unpleasant and has made people "invent" things like siesta to use the day in the best possible way, argues Landes. Third, Landes argues that the climate of tropical regions such as those of Africa have the side effect of being a very good environment for parasites and diseases. This is especially true in sub-Saharan Africa, where a cleansing frost like the one that the temperate climates gets, is not present. The rain cycles of sub-Saharan Africa are much more varied, irregular and heavier than in Northwestern Europe. Hence, for Landes (1998), Africa's underdevelopment is a result of its own geography and climatic conditions.

Foreign aid and dependency syndrome

For other scholars such as Moyo (2009), foreign aid is the major stumbling block for Africa's developmental jump. This is because foreign aid has cultivated dependency syndrome. Dependency syndrome is generally an attitude and belief by an individual or group that they cannot solve their own problems without outside help (Bartle 1967). This means that where there is dependency syndrome, there is lack of self- reliance and relegation of internal factors as irrelevant to initiate and foster development. Also, where there is always foreign aid, there is no learning (Easterly 2008). Easterly give examples of problems that were diagnosed in 1938 only to be found recurring by 2005. In his research on such problems, Easterly (Ibid: 31) noted that "Hailey report of 1938 vs. UN Millennium project of 2005 found out the same problems namely: malaria, hunger, nutrition, soil fertility, soil erosion and deforestation, land tenure, clean drinking water" to have remained unsolved in Africa. This has largely been believed to be a result of foreign aid dependency, such that some scholars have considered aid as a curse – "Aid curse." It is also for the same reason that some scholars have argued that the formal withdrawal at African independence of Western colonial governments and states never resulted in substantive decolonisation as Western corporations, institutions and governments continue to be operational on the continent.

Investment in faith instead of science and technology

The decades 80s and 90s have seen the international community increasingly acknowledging that science and technology play a leading role in fostering development. In Africa, this role had been submerged in the previous two decades as the focus shifted to poverty-reduction strategies *and faith* without recognising that the strategies required significant input of scientific knowledge (Dickson 2006). In Zimbabwe, this investment in faith is evidenced by the mushrooming of churches known as Africa Initiated Churches. For Dickson, it is unfortunate that Africa has invested more in faith than it has done in science and technology yet the later are the drivers of development. And, to leap frog from underdevelopment to development, Africa need to invest more in science and technology than it does in faith. No wonder Dickson (2006) underlined that: "science and technology are essential to address problems of health and hunger, and to provide jobs by boosting economic growth, but this needs to be more than an argument of faith" (p. 5).

Conclusion

As has been discussed in this chapter, the idea whether Africa's underdevelopment is a plight of its own making is highly contentious: it can neither be answered in a word nor dismissed by a wave of hand. Basing on this understanding, the present chapter has discussed the notion in question paying particular attention to the different interpretations and arguments proffered through time in view of underdevelopment, thereby revealing the controversies surrounding the notion and in some places, articulating how these "turbulent waters" could possibly be manoeuvred and navigated through.

Yet, although it is argued in this chapter, and indeed the whole book, that externally initiated episodes of trans-Atlantic slave trade, capitalism, colonialism and neo-colonialism, among other factors, have played a pivotal role in sowing and watering the seed of underdevelopment in Africa, one can be tempted to conclude that the underdevelopment of Africa is largely a plight of its own making, especially if we are to consider lack of framework of development, corruption, poor governance and lack of political will visible in many Africa governments: Africans are in fact not doing enough to resist the caprices and whims of externally initiated underdevelopment on the continent.

Chapter 4

Development, Underdevelopment and Globalisation in Africa

"If anything, modern globalisation is a bitter pill that one takes with a crinkle face" (Munyaradzi Mawere 2013).

Introduction

Elsewhere, I have argued in view of African cultures, norms and values that if anything, modern globalisation is a bitter pill that one takes with a crinkle face. I have gone further to argue that a bitter pill has a double effect – it heals while paining – but sometimes it pains while it doesn't heal at all. So is globalisation? The globalisation question in this book is, however, not applied to issues of culture, norms and values, but to issues of development and underdevelopment in Africa. The grand question is: shall we equally consider globalisation as a bitter pill that one takes with a crinkle face when it comes to issues of development and underdevelopment in Africa? Also, is globalisation a tonic to Africa's development or else it is a wreck spat designed to overturn the development fortunes of the continent? Or still, is globalisation a lethal pill that is meant to deepen the sleep of the giant lion – Africa – so that it will never wake up?

In a bid to think through the questions highlighted above, it will be important to first and foremost problematise the term "globalisation," which in fact, though has gained tremendous prominence in intellectual discourse over the years in both Africa and beyond, remains peculiarly difficult to unpack and pin down with precision as far as its historiography and conceptualisation are concerned. Such problematisation is not only important for the mere reason that globalisation as a term has become too philosophical, but also because the term is elastic and pragmatic such that it cuts across contexts and different historical. The tenuous nature coupled with the different versions of historiographies of globalisation, necessitates a vigorous meticulous interrogation of the term both as a phenomenon and a process of change with practical manifestations and applications in particularly situated contexts such as those of Africa.

In view of these important observations, the present chapter attempts to unpack globalisation especially as it relates to development (or underdevelopment) of Africa and also applies to contexts such as those of the so-called developing countries (also known as Third World countries) such as those of Africa. In this whole attempt, the chapter also goes a step further to critically evaluates the assertion whether globalisation in Africa is functionally an old phenomenon and qualitatively a new phrase or not.

Understanding globalisation

As highlighted above, the term "globalisation" and the discourse surrounding it are highly momentous and have sustained controversies of epic proportions in both theory and practice. In some contexts, the meaning and history of globalisation have been often assumed, taken for granted, loosely and uncritically applied while in others globalisation has been described with chariness and criticality. Resultantly, globalisation has come to mean different things to different people depending on their orientation, prompting the term to become the latest buzzword and assume different definitions and interpretations both conceptually and historically: it has indeed become "the cliché of our times" (Held *et al* 1999:6). For some scholars, globalisation has come to mean "a process in which business decisions, production processes, and markets gradually exhibit more international characteristics and less national ones" (Waller-Hunter & Jones 2002: 53). For Third World Economics Trends and Analysis Report (1997), globalisation refers to a process of increasing economic openness, growing economic interdependence and deepening economic integration between countries of the world. Albrow and King (1990: 8) conceptualise globalisation as "all processes by which the peoples of the world are interconnected (through interaction) and incorporated into a single world society." And, for Jagdish (2004: 3), globalisation is typically an economic process whereby local "[national] economies are integrated into the international economy through trade, foreign direct investment, capital flows, migration and the spread of technology."

It should be underscored that all the aforementioned interpretations of globalisation are flawed in a way. They either view globalisation as a positive process of change or are narrow in so far as they emphasise trade, which is the main driver of globalisation, while silent of other important drivers such as technology and the United Nations liberalisation policy. Besides, they also do not underline the possible negative effects (on cultures, economies, politics, environments and religions) of the process of globalisation on developing countries (as those of Africa). Yet, it is on the basis of the negatives associated with [modern] globalisation in view of the Developing World that some scholars have described it as "a bitter pill that one takes with a crinkle face" (Mawere 2013; Mawere 2016: 1-2), and others describe it as "the latest stage of imperialism" (Bello 2003; see also L5L 2003), and more others conceive it as "Euro-American imperialism" (Aborishade 2002) that results in either "cultural atrophy" (Ekwuru 1999) or "cultural crisis" (Akindele 2002). On realising the narrowness of many of the definitions proffered in view of globalisation, Lawal (2006) has come to understand it [globalisation] more holistically as "a process of integrating not only the economies of nations but also their culture, technology, knowledge, politics and governance." In more or less similar terms, Zivenge (2016) has come to understand globalisation generally as the interaction and integration among the world communities, powered by technology and facilitated by policy, but induced by international trade. What Zivenge seems to overlook in his interpretation of globalisation, however, is the fact that globalisation has a double effect. It is a force that can tear the communities of the world apart and a force that binds the communities of the world together. I call this the paradox of globalisation. It should be underscored, however, that the definition of globalisation as both a concept and a process remains highly contentious and difficult to state in a word.

However, from Zivenge's interpretation, one notes that there are three main drivers of globalisation namely: international trade, technology, and the United Nations liberalisation policy, of which the last two are qualitatively new without which globalisation as known today could have been impossible or rather slower than is. Moreover, one notes that globalisation *ideally* speaking primarily increases human interaction while secondarily promotes human integration and ultimately aims at developing the human society and improving human life. In other words, the primary goal of globalisation is increasing human interaction across the world. On the same note, human interaction in turn results in human integration whereby people of different [world] societies develop tolerance to live at peace with each other, continuing with the interaction process socially, politically and economically. This integration of human societies [or people of the world] ultimately results in the ultimate goal of globalisation which is development of all human societies, hence the reason why globalisation, ideally speaking, has as its ultimate goal the development of human societies.

Globalisation in history

As underlined in the introduction of this chapter, the historical origin of globalisation, as that of development which it allegedly aims to promote, is a subject of ongoing debate. There are two major contesting parties, with one situating the origins of globalisation in the modern era and the other party regarding it as a long time phenomenon as old as human history.

Starting with those who situate globalisation in the golden age, they generally argue that dissociating globalisation from history gives us a smudged false picture of world socio-economic systems. For them, globalisation is inherent to human co-existence and indeed an integral part of human history such that the history of the world has always been associated with the process of globalisation at different degrees of intensity relative to their socio-economic and political conditions at different times. One of the chief proponents of a deep historical origin of globalisation was the Economist associated with dependency theory, Andre Gunder Frank. Defending his position, Frank (1998) argues that globalisation has always been in existence in the olden days, particularly since the rise of trade links between Sumer and the Indus Valley Civilisation, such that to say globalisation is functionally a new phenomenon is a misnomer. This period was in the third millennium B.C. To corroborate Frank's position, one could even go further to argue that even as early as the so-called "Prehistoric period", globalisation was already taking place with territorial expansion from the cradle of mankind – Africa – by our ancestors to all five continents being the initial step towards the establishment of globalisation. The existence of the Jawara people – people of African origin – believed to have been "trapped" for centuries now on the Andaman Island of India also testify that globalisation is an old phenomenon (Mawere & Mubaya 2016). The process [of globalisation] was, however, propelled by the agricultural and industrial revolutions and later on by population explosion, technological advancements and scarcity of resources after the First and Second World Wars. These factors led to the need liberalise world economies by opening up more boundaries for exchange of goods, ideas and services across the world, thereby magnifying the intensity of globalisation. The discovery of new markets in the 19th and 20th centuries, in turn, prompted the need to advance in technology – communication and transport – to facilitate and speed up the movement of goods and services from one part of the world to another (cf. O'Rourke *et al* 2000). The intensification of globalisation during this period grew faster than before through the intersection of four interrelated sets of communities of practice namely academics, journalists, publishers and libraries (James & Steger 2014). Thus, for Frank as with O'Rourke *et al*, Mawere and Mubaya, James and Steger, globalisation is not functionally a new phenomenon but simply a new phase qualitatively: globalisation has always been there with all its drivers – trade, technology and policy – existent though in varying degrees.

While Frank's argument is difficult to dislodge given that he offers historical evidence to substantiate his claim, his critics contend that Frank's idea rests upon an over-broad and general definition of globalisation. Frank, thus, has been accused of being too general. One of his critics, Thomas Friedman, for example, has argued that although globalisation is an old aged phenomenon functionally, it should not be overgeneralised to mean one and the same thing as it mean today: globalisation has qualitatively changed. Friedman (2005) goes a step further to divide the history of globalisation into three distinct periods namely: Globalisation 1 (stretching from 1492–1800), Globalisation 2 (stretching from 1800–2000) and Globalisation 3 (stretching from 2000 to the present time). For Friedman, Globalisation 1 involved the globalisation [or interaction] of countries as pioneered by explorers such as Christopher Columbus, Bartholomew Dias, Marco Polo, and Vasco da Gama, among others (cf. Mawere 2014). Globalisation 2 involved the globalisation of companies such as the British South African Company and many other such multi-national companies and organisations, while Globalisation 3 involves the globalisation of individuals as they move from one part of the world to the other in search of good life – greener pastures, trading and visiting friends and relatives. Friedman's three phases of globalisation are more or less the same as Yaman's (2001) three stages of globalisation namely: 1) Stage 1: Colonialism (1490s – 1890s); 2) Stage 2: Imperialism (1890s – 1990s) and; 3) Regional and economic integration (1990s – present). Thus for Friedman as with Yaman, globalisation is not functionally a new phenomenon but qualitatively a new phase that has increased human interaction given that their second and third phases/stages have been largely driven by secondary drivers – technology and international policy of liberalisation – which are indeed qualitatively new phases in the globalisation matrix.

Adela Lee (n.d) gives an almost similar characterisation of globalisation as Friedman and Yaman, yet he looks at globalisation from an economic and cultural perspective. For Lee, globalisation in the Western world started as early as the Hellenistic Age when an early form of globalised economics and culture known as "archaic globalisation" existed. For him, archaic globalisation, which stretched up to the 16th century, allowed commercialised urban centres around the axis of Greek civilisation to stretch over a wide area, from India to Spain, with cities such as Athens, Alexandria and Antioch at the centre of this form of globalisation. This form of globalisation was facilitated by widespread trade and later developments in transport and communication, which for the first time saw the idea of a cosmopolitan culture (from Greek 'Cosmopolis', meaning 'world city') emerging. As Lee further notes, another early form of globalisation facilitated by trade between the Roman Empire, the Parthian Empire and the Han Dynasty, increased commercial links between these powers leading to the development of the Silk Road. The Silk Road started in western China, stretching up to the boundaries of the Parthian Empire and to Rome.

On a similar note, Hobson (2004) notes that the Islamic Golden Age when Jews and Muslim traders and explorers established a sustained economy across the Old World was also an important early stage of globalisation. It gave birth to globalisation of crops such as sugar, banana and cotton as well as knowledge, language (particularly Arabic), technology and trade. This first phase of globalisation, which was characterised by the rise of maritime European empires in the 16th and 17th centuries, started with the Portuguese and Spanish empires, and later the Dutch and British empires. This phase also witnessed the founding of chartered companies like British East India Company founded in 1600 and often described as the first multinational corporation. This was followed by the Dutch East India Company founded in 1602. It also led to the age of discovery and to the third and present phase of globalisation known as modern globalisation, which started in the 19th century and shaped by industrialisation and European imperialism. In essence, for scholars like Lee and Hobson (2004), these pre-modern phases of global exchange are a clear testimony that globalisation is not functionally a new phenomenon but only qualitatively a new phase.

More so, critical analysis of socio-economic and political events across the world show that globalisation, a highly controversial and complex concept-cum-process, is not functionally a new phenomenon but simply a continuation of developments that have been taking place for quite a long time before. It should be acknowledged, however, that the recent trend of globalisation especially of economic and cultural activities is qualitatively different or rather new. From an economic perspective, for example, the world is no longer a collection of relatively independent economic agents that are only marginally connected. Economic agents, especially those from the developing world, are now more or less immune to economic events in their neighbourhood. Mrak (2000: v) captures this aptly when he observes:

> Today, globalisation involves numerous features, but the following are the main engine driving global economic integration: a) internationalisation of production accompanied by changes in the structure of production, b) expansion of international trade in trade and services, and c) widening and deepening of international capital flows.

Understood in this sense, one could notice that globalisation is a forceful process that is now more resilient than ever and unlikely to be reversed. In fact, as Lawal (2006: 65) assertively argues, since the whole process is about development and transformation "the process of globalisation has become the necessary consequence of the economic development, which is the pursuit of most modern market economies leading to interconnectedness of most economies" such that no country can now afford to be dormant as a nation with a closed economy. Thus, although globalisation is not functionally a new phenomenon, it is qualitatively a new phase especially when taking into cognisance the formidable unification and re-shaping of the world into a "global village" (to use McLuhan's 1960 term) as well as the dynamics of socio-economic and political relations the world-over.

For the hyper-globalisers such as scholars like Olimae and Lawal (2006), globalisation is seen as a new period in which people everywhere are increasingly subject of the disciplines of the global marketplace, that is, an era of human history in which traditional nation states have become unnatural, smoothening impossible business units in a global economy. This therefore presents an economic logic with the emergence of a single global market and the principle of global competition as the harbingers of human progress (Held *et al* 1999). For Musa Ibrahim (n.d: 8), this makes the economic dimension of globalisation as known today, a historically old phenomenon but qualitatively a new phase given that it is "the most formidable and driving force for the political and social aspects" of global relations. Ibrahim (Ibid) gives an example of colonialism with which "European cultures *through the use of technology as a drive* found their ways into other parts of the world through the colonisation of colonies which was spurred by the industrial revolution in Europe with the logic of the colonisation process being to create a more integrated world economy controlled by the metropolitan countries." Thus for Olimae as with Lawal and Ibrahim, globalisation though functionally not a new phenomenon it is qualitatively a new phase that focuses more on international reflection of the co-existence and interdependence nature of humanity.

Yet, while those who situate globalisation in the golden age generally argue that dissociating globalisation from history gives us an encrusted false picture of world economic systems, scholars who situate it in the modern era generally argue that stretching the beginning of globalisation far back in time renders the concept wholly inoperative and useless for political analysis (Daniele 2010). For these later scholars, globalisation is a modern or contemporary phenomenon. Fairoozi Hamdi (2015: 1) who subscribe to this school of thought, for example, argues that "the history of globalisation *only* goes back to the second half of the twentieth century: the development of transport and communication technology led to a situation where national borders appeared to be too limiting for economic activity." What Hamdi alludes to is that whatever processes took place before the second half of the twentieth century, was not globalisation in its strict and functional sense. This kind of reasoning finds favour in Hardt and Negri (2000) who consider events and processes that took place before the second half of the twentieth century as nothing less than imperialism and not globalisation per se. Hardt and Negri (2000) understand imperialism, thus, as "an extension of the sovereignty of the European nation-states beyond their own boundaries" (p. xii). The duo believes that the so-called globalisation is in fact an extension of what Lenin identified as imperialism. Georges Labica (2007) corroborates the same line of thinking arguing that:

> The features of imperialism identified by Lenin have been continued, but they are accelerated by the conjunction of three recent phenomena: the predominance of speculative finance capital, the technological revolutions, especially in the field of information and communications, and the collapse of the so-called socialist countries (p. 229).

William Robinson (2004) also agrees that what we call globalisation today should not be understood as such. For him, it should be better understood as 'global capitalism' as it is characterised by "a transition from the nation state phase of world capitalism to a transnational phase" (p. 5). In view of the prevailing globalisation process, this creates unequal relationships between the so-called developed and developing countries. Stiglitz (2002: 12) summarises this unequal relationship aptly when he argues:

> Today, few-apart from those with vested interests who benefit from keeping out the goods produced by the poor countries-defend the hypocrisy of pretending to help developing

countries by forcing them to open up their markets to the goods of the advanced industrial countries while keeping their own markets protected, policies that make the rich richer and the poor more impoverished-and increasingly angry.

Taking it from this sense and from Hardt, Negri, Labica, Hamdi and Robinson's arguments elaborated above, if we look at the intention of all the events and processes that took place before what we now call *globalisation* such as trans-Atlantic slave, imperialism, capitalism and colonialism, we note that they were meant to dominate other peoples and their territories and not to harmonise different communities in socio-economic and political terms as globalisation today ideally preaches. Thus for Hardt, Negri, Labica and Hamdi, globalisation understood ideally as the mutual interaction and integration among world's communities facilitated by three drivers namely international trade, technological advancement and international liberal policy, is both a functionally new phenomenon and a qualitatively new phase.

Globalisation and [under-]development in Africa

The pillaging and plundering of Africa, both its human capital and raw materials continues! Incidences of human trafficking and looting of resources from Africa to overseas countries of Europe are more than ubiquitous now that globalisation allows easier movement of people and goods. The questions that continue haunting us are many: Why Africa has remained a target for exploitation for this long? Is it because Africa is too rich with beautiful resources that attract the eyes of the predators? How can this plundering be stopped once and for all when globalisation continues opening its doors for the entrance of trafficked humans and looted goods? How can this plundering be stopped when the predatory mind-set of those who benefit from exploiting other people's resources has not changed and worse still have become more empowered by the tools of globalisation such as information communication technology? How can this plundering be stopped when globalisation nurtures the Global North to emerge as the unchallengeable winner that continue to dominate world affairs and impose its interests on all others whom it depicts as pitiable, voiceless, and desperate "others" who need nothing but the North's salvation?

Surprisingly, globalisation has always been defined by its proponents as a process of change meant to foster and propel the development locus of the world. This way, globalisation has been perceived by some as a positive process that has yielded [and continue to yield] good results in many societies of the world, especially the so-called developing countries of the world such as Africa. Some of the positive impacts of globalisation as argued by proponents of globalisation include:

Liberalisation of economies

One of the benefits of globalisation has been liberalisation of world economies. Liberalisation of economies entails the creation of interdependent free markets to achieve higher efficiency and provide Gross Domestic Products (GDP) growth in underdeveloped regions. With globalisation, there has been lifting up of stringent regulations on trade which formerly limited world economies to do business with each other. It is through globalisation, for that we witness the formation of World Trade Organisation (WTO) to promote trade at global level. Liberation of economies itself has brought forth a numerous advantages which include but not limited to stimulation of economic growth, generation of a wider range of products, creation of democratic political and economic systems, and provision of a wide range of products and services on the market at a fairly lower cost.

Increase in wealth

It is also argued by proponents of globalisation that globalisation has increased wealth in formerly underdeveloped countries. As Boundless (2016) reveals, per capita GDP growth rates in developing countries have been stimulated by globalisation. Boundless gives an example of the 1960s where non-globalised economies grew at an annual rate of 1. 4 % while globalised economies grew at 4. 7 %. Boundless provides another example of the 1990s when developing economies that had just globalised grew at 5. 0% annually as compared to only 2. 2% annual growth in economies that had globalised for longer. The correlation between globalisation and annual growth as has been shown above demonstrate the benefits of globalisation. Thus, globalisation has the merit that it increases world people's wealth while reducing international poverty.

Better quality of life
While globalisation has been widely criticised on moral, cultural and religious grounds, it has arguably improved the quality of life of the world communities. In fact, the widespread availability of global goods, services and ideas has positively impacted on the lives of the people at a world scale. Boundless (2016) identify some of the different areas where advocates claim globalisation to be benefitting people as:

- More opportunities for international travel and tourism.
- Better access to external financing such as house and car loans.
- Greater consumption of worldwide entertainment including music, sports, and pop culture.
- More opportunities to work abroad due to liberal immigrant laws and foreign worker programmes.
- The rapid spread of consumer goods such as clothing, foods, vehicles, and global telecommunication infrastructure and technologies such as internet and mobile phones.

Communication
Along with the benefit on bettering human life discussed above, globalisation has brought about great strides in the areas of communication. As argued by Gibbons (2000), globalisation is a blessing given that it has improved communication through internet, skype, phones, telegram and other such social media avenues. Via

these communication channels, distance between people is no longer a big concern. People who live miles apart, for example, can now afford to chat with each other via skype. They can now afford to talk to one another via mobile telephones. They can now afford to send messages to each other via internet and so on. Thus, globalisation contributes to the spreading of technologies as those in the areas of telecommunications.

Educational

Scholars like Gibbons (2000) and Scott (1994) argue that due to globalisation the university across the world is becoming uniformly transformed with inter-disciplinarity being emphatically underlined. Besides, globalisation has brought with it liberalised international study programmes which allow students from one country to go and study in other countries. Though such programmes, a student from Mozambique, for example, can go and study in the United States of America and vice versa. In the past decade, Zimbabwe has also witnessed more and more of its students leaving the country to study in neighbouring countries such as South Africa and Botswana. This has become easier because with globalisation people can now move across borders to different parts of the world to acquire the education they aspire. This has, in a way, resulted in the integration of cultures.

However, as a process dictated mainly by the Global North, globalisation has been accused of causing pandemonium and problems of serious magnitudes to societies mainly in the Global South such as those of Africa. It is on the same basis that elsewhere (Mawere 2013), I critiqued globalisation in view of its negative effects on the cultures, religions and social norms and values of the Global South to the extent that I labelled it "a bitter pill that one takes with a crinkle face". Considering further the negative effects of globalisation on the economies of the Global South, I add that globalisation is an old imperialism or evolved colonialism that comes in the guise of promoting development: it is a rayon glove covering an iron fist that does not only grab but squeezes hard and prickles or even worse, it is a wolf playing sheep. I should be audacious here to underscore that the wolf in this case is the Global North while the sheep is the Global South which is preyed on by the former. Leaving this aside, I move on to discuss some of the negative impacts of globalisation that have been raised in relation to societies of the Global South:

Denigration of culture

For scholars like Ekwuru (1999), globalisation has resulted in cultural atrophy, that is, death of other cultures. For others like Akandele (2002), globalisation has caused cultural crisis in many societies of Africa, leading other scholars such as Aborishade (2002) to argue that globalisation is nothing less than cultural, political and economic domination. Thus, for all these scholars, globalisation has negatively affected cultures of the subaltern societies, particularly those of Africa where cultural uniqueness is increasingly being lost in favour of homogenisation and "universal culture," which in any case happen to be the culture of the metropole, particularly the North America and Europe. The domination of foreign culture of the North in the South has prompted a plethora of social problems ranging from individualism to loss of respect for elders, from poaching to human organ trading, from drug abuse to human trafficking, and from family destabilisation to family disintegration.

Ruin of local economies

While proponents of globalisation argue that globalisation can reduce international poverty, it can also be argued that the same process ruins local economies, particularly those of developing countries. The establishment of multinational companies in the developing countries has, for example, witnessed many competing local companies in those countries closing their businesses as they fail to withstand competition. On this note, it can be argued that globalisation is only good for the so-called First World Countries of the Global North which can competitively sell more products and establish big companies in Third World countries in the guise of globalisation. A very good example is the big American brands such as McDonald and Starbucks which have dominated many Third World countries ousting local brands in these poorer countries. This stifles development of underdeveloped countries while help increasing the gap between the poor and the rich countries.

Globalisation increases world carbon gasses emissions

Carbon dioxide emissions are the major causes of the destruction of the ozone layer and climate change. In fact between 1987 and 1997, emissions rose at an average of 1 % per year which meant that emissions in 2011 would have risen to 18 % if nothing was done at a global scale (Tverberg 2013). This realisation prompted the formulation of the 1997 Kyoto Protocol world countries so as to arrest further deterioration of the ozone layer while controlling climatic change conditions. Unfortunately, even with the Kyoto Protocol in place nothing much has changed as emissions from developed countries of the North and China continue to rise. Developing countries are also joining in, thereby complicating the problem even further. In Africa in the past five years for example, Zimbabwe has become one of the motor-vehicle consumers of the car industry in Japan; something that could have been impossible without globalisation. This has, however, has witnessed increased levels of carbon gasses in Zimbabwe over the past few years.

Globalisation widens the gap between the poor and the rich

Related to the point above is the argument by anti-globalisation proponents that globalisation results in the widening of the gap between the poor and the rich. Bahl (2016) is apt to observe that 86 % of the world's resources are said to be consumed by the richest 20 % of the world population, which means that the poorer 80 % only gets to consume 14 % of the world's resources. This is a direct consequence of globalisation which has opened the doors of all world markets to everyone. Also, as Yusuf and Watkins (cited in McCubbrey 2016) observe, the growth of international trade in the name of globalisation is exacerbating income inequalities, both between and within industrialised and less industrialised nations. This is because global commerce is increasingly dominated by large transnational corporations which seek nothing except maximising profits without regard for development needs of individual countries and peoples. Besides, protectionist policies in the so-called First World or industrialised countries prevent many producers in Third World countries from accessing export markets (cf. McCubbrey 2016). These protectionist policies seem to be operational at both local and international levels, which gives room for the widening of the gap between the poor and the rich within the developing countries themselves and between people of developed and developing countries. Thus, it is safe to argue that globalisation only serves the interests of the rich while the poor are made to face all its negative effects.

Globalisation uses up finite resources more quickly

As argued by Tverberg (2013), globalisation seems to be looked on as an unlimited "good" by economists who unfortunately seem to be misguided by flawed models to think that the world is finite. Yet the truth is we do not have infinite resources. Neither do we have unlimited ability to handle properly those finite resources at our disposal. This, combined with the fact that where markets are open everyone is free to come and exploit the resource on the market, possess a big threat to finite resources that we have on earth. Tverberg gives a good example of China, which she notes joined the World Trade Organisation (WTO) in 2001, yet by 2002 its coal use had already began rising rapidly. India experienced a similar problem with its coal reserves. Thus, with globalisation's open door policy, finite resources (also known as non-renewable resources) are used up more quickly than would be the case in non-globalised countries.

Rapid spread of diseases

Globalisation has increased mobility at a global scale. This increased mobility has resulted in the rapid spread of deadly diseases such as HIV/AIDS and other communicable diseases such as Ebola, hepatitis B, measles, rabies, tuberculosis, and Zika, among others via travellers and business operators. In the past few decades, all the aforementioned diseases have spread from one part of the world to another much easier as a result of globalisation.

Rise in crime rate

Over the past few years, there has been a sharp rise in the world crime rate. This rise has largely been a result of globalisation which has facilitated the formation and linkages of criminal syndicates operating from different parts of the world. Such syndicates are very difficult to deal with due to liberalised migration laws. Today, we have syndicates dealing with drug trafficking, robbery, human organ trading, human trafficking and other such crimes across the world, yet dealing with them effectively remains a thorn in the flesh.

Conclusion

As revealed in this chapter, "globalisation" both as a concept and a process of change, has been used in many ways such that it has formed the basis of confusion and controversy entrenched in the historiographical and conceptual understanding of the full grasp of what the term actually entails. While some perceive globalisation as an enduring process that is possibly as old as human history itself, others consider it as both functionally and qualitatively a new phase. It is on this basis that this chapter has argued that the assertion whether globalisation is functionally an old phenomenon and qualitatively a new phrase or not cannot be responded to in a word but by critically and reflectively looking at the historiography of globalisation and the different approaches to the globalisation discourse in general. Yet, drawing on the arguments proffered in this chapter around the historiography of globalisation, it can be concluded that globalisation is *not* functionally a new phenomenon, but *only* qualitatively a new phase.

At another level, I have discussed the viability and impact of globalisation in contemporary societies of Africa. On this note, I have audaciously criticised globalisation and challenged theorists of development in the Global South to embark on a bold programme of development based on the notion of democratic fair strategic plan that deconstruct and reconstruct globalisation for it to make a meaningful benefit to the South and its people. In fact, I have made a clarion call to theorists of development in the Global South to take a stand in our own sphere of influence and at minimum not to support the ongoing plunder of the South's precious resources by the North. I, thus, have evoked the resistance against such all asymmetrical relationships between the South and the North and discourses that divert the South's energy from creating and building. For me, this is the truth that has to be told. I therefore conclude this chapter by challenging theorists of development in and on the South that the time has ripen: it is now that we should do more talking and writing other than leaving development theorists from the North to continue doing so on our behalf.

Chapter 5

Poverty and Inequality: Unpacking the Pragmatics of Poverty and Inequality in Africa

"Poverty will remain forever at the core of all human problems as long as we live in an unequal society" (Munyaradzi Mawere 2016).

Introduction

For a long time now, poverty has always remained at the centre of all the problems that haunt Africa. One of the major problems that co-exist with poverty is inequality. Unfortunately, it seems the dominance of the poverty problem will persist many years to come if not forever. This observation comes along as the enduring problems of poverty and food shortage as a result of population explosion, rising in cost of living and changing climatic conditions, among other reasons, have over the years prompted many governments, scholars, researchers and theorists to seek permanent solutions that foster development at a world scale, but in vain.

In the areas of development economics or agriculture in general, many theories and models of development such as Lewis' theory of trickle-down effect and Fei-Ranis' dual economy model, among others, have been postulated in an attempt to ward off poverty while influencing development and reducing the inequality gap especially in the so-called developing countries. For purposes of this chapter, critical analysis of poverty, but with a particular focus on Africa, is made before the relationship between poverty and inequality is explicated. The second part of the chapter goes a step further to discuss the different theories of poverty and how these try to explain the development process taking place in many African countries. This is then followed by the conclusion that is drawn from the discussion.

Understanding poverty

While scholars generally agree that poverty is ubiquitous on the face of the world especially in the so-called developing countries, the term "poverty" has never been easy to define, at least with precision. The difficulty in unpacking what poverty entails mainly emanates from the fact that although many people are said to be living in or under poverty conditions, what to one is poverty is in fact not poverty to another. Put differently, the understanding of poverty largely depends on who defines it and how. The conceptualisation of poverty in the African framework, for example, may differ from the conceptualisation of the same in the European framework. So is how it [poverty] is measured in both the African and the European frameworks. On the basis of these two frameworks, one may discover that s/he is poor in view of the European framework but rich in view of the African framework. Thus poverty is not only difficult to define but also difficult to measure.

Nevertheless many definitions of poverty have been conjured throughout history. Sen (1999), for example, in his book: *Development as Freedom*, shifts his understanding from poverty in general terms as the lack of basic necessities to deprivation of human capabilities. What Sen means here is that poverty implies that people cannot afford: they lack. It is a situation of lack. For Sen, a lack of basic necessities such as shelter, education, clothing, food, employment opportunities, medical care and social security entails poverty; more importantly they deprive one's ability to capitalise on his/her own capabilities as free human agents. While this definition directs us to what many can believe to be signs (or symptoms) of poverty, it should be underlined that what one considers as a necessity is relative. So is need and freedom: what one may consider as a need or an expression of freedom, as Sen himself tells us, is dependent of social definition and past experience. Yet what Sen tells us is important in that he recognise freedom as both an "end" and a "means" of development. What this means is that where poverty prevails, there is no freedom. On this note, I add on what Sen argues to advance that poverty and injustice are inseparable. The moment we eradicate poverty, we have conquered injustice in our land. But as long as poverty persists, gross injustice will also live longer with us. This is because eradication of poverty does not only entail casting off of one's chains of poverty. It is affording power and opportunity for one to advance self and collective desires while controlling one's person with diligence and discipline.

Following the footsteps of Sen, Narayan *et al* (2000: 4-5) define poverty as multidimensional deprivation that "includes hunger, illiteracy, illness and poor health, powerlessness, voicelessness, insecurity, humiliation, and lack of access to basic infrastructure." Similarly, Ramlogan (2004: 140) asserts that "poverty, in its most extreme form, is the condition that exists when people lack the means to fulfil basic human needs, adequate and nutritious food, clothing, housing, clean water, and health services." What Narayan *et al* and Ramlogan are saying implies that the identification of poor people in Africa first requires a determination of what constitutes basic needs. We can only determine whether one lives in poverty or not after delineating what constitute basic needs and whether these can be met or not.

Other scholars such as Valentine, however, look at poverty from a legal perspective. For Valentine (1968), the essential characteristic of poverty in any given society is inequality. Thus, for him, no matter how rich a society could claim to be, as long as there is a wide gap between the rich and the poor, that society is characterised by poverty.

The United Nations (UN) has tried to come up with an all-encompassing definition of poverty that could possibly be applicable in all contexts of the world. For the UN (2000), poverty is "a human condition characterised by the sustained or chronic deprivation of the resources, capabilities, choices, security and power necessary for the enjoyment of an adequate standard of living and other civil, cultural, economic, political and social rights". However, while the UN's definition seems to be all encompassing, it emphasises more on the legal grounding of poverty as a phenomenon. Besides, what one refers to as "adequate standard of living" is always relative, differing from one individual (or society) to another.

The variation of definitions of poverty could be explained in terms of history. Rowntree's study in 1901 marks the first step towards the development of a poverty standard for individual families, based on estimates of nutritional and other such requirements he deemed necessary for a "steady" life. This understanding of poverty shifted in the mid-1950s when the main focus was now on the level of income reflected in macro-economic indicators such as Gross National Product (GNP) per head. By the 1970s, poverty studies had become prominent, with poverty understood not only as a failure to meet minimum nutrition or subsistence levels, but rather a failure to keep up with the pace and standard of life in a given society. By the mid-1970s, poverty came to be defined not only as lack of income, but also lack of access to education, health facilities, clean water, decent accommodation and other such services. The understanding of poverty as has been seen in the different definitions discussed above has always been changing from time to time. What remains clear is that when we talk of poverty, we talk of reduced, incapacitated, or complete lack of access to all that can make human life worth living. Basing on this understanding, poverty is understood in this book as the partial or complete lack of access to all that makes human life worth living. By this I mean when one lacks (either partially or completely) the access to this that makes him/her leading a happy life or desirable life – a life worth living – that person is poor. These things are noted here as resources capitals in the form of material, economic, cultural, social, political and religious needs as it is all these facets that make one's life not only complete but desirable and worth living. A lack of any one of the aforementioned variables is likely to incapacitate the individual in question, hence hampering that person from living a desirable life.

In the contemporary times, poverty has come to be viewed in both relative and absolute terms hence; we have what is known simply as relative poverty and absolute poverty. For many years, the World Bank has defined absolute poverty as the condition of not having the means to afford basic human needs with the one involved living below the US$1/day line. Due to depreciation of the US$, the poverty datum line per day has increased from US$1/day to US$1, 25/day. On the other hand, relative poverty is a condition of having fewer resources (or income) than others in a given society. In other words, relative poverty is calculated by comparing the highest segment of a given population with the lowest segment. Thus in a society (say A) where we have two members (X who is richer and P who is poor as compared to X), we can deduce, using such calculations, that P in society A is relatively poor than X in the same society. Mowafi (n.d: 3) summarises the distinction between absolute poverty and relative poverty more aptly when he says "while absolute poverty refers to the set of resources a person must acquire in order to maintain a minimum standard of living, relative poverty is concerned with how well off an individual is with respect to others in the same society." This means that while the measure of absolute poverty may, in theory, be expected to remain stable, relative poverty line is expected to shift over time as the overall standard of living in a given society changes.

Inequality and poverty

Inequality generally refers to a condition of being unequal between and amongst members of the same society which creates imbalanced (or uneven) opportunities to access resources such as shelter, land, clothing, food and others. Inequality could be social, economic or some other ways that exclude other people from benefitting from a given resource. This means that inequality breeds disparity, difference, and discrepancies between and amongst people leading into comparisons such as poor and rich. It is on this note that many scholars perceive inequality as the obverse of poverty.

I have highlighted in the preceding section that although sometimes appear invisible and difficult to measure, poverty is measurable. Poverty is normally measured using poverty indicators, which are both qualitative and quantitative. To measure poverty in a country, we look at the poverty datum line. By poverty datum line (PDL), I mean a representation of the cost of a given standard of living that must be attained if a person is deemed not to be poor (Zimbabwe's Ministry of Finance and Economic Development 2014). One may however be poor in terms of food provision and not poor in terms of other provisions such as clothing and shelter, hence we also what we call food poverty datum line (FPDL), which represents the minimum consumption expenditure necessary to ensure that each household member can (if all expenditures were devoted to food) consume a minimum food basket representing 2 100 calories (Ibid). This means that any individual (or household) whose total consumption expenditure does not exceed the poverty line is judged to be poor. In Zimbabwe, the national food poverty line (FPL) per person as at January 2014 stood at US$32. 00 as compared to US$31. 00 of December 2013 (Ibid). This means that the minimum needs basket cost per person in January 2014 was $32. 00 as of January 2014. Currently, Zimbabwe's poverty datum line is pegged at US$500. 00 with percentage of the poor being 90 % while that of the rich stands at 10 % as compared to the 75 % (poor people) and 25 % (rich people) during the colonial period. What this means is that all people earning US$ 499. 00 and below are deemed poor but poverty levels remain varied as we have other people earning say US $ 150. 00, others earning US $ 250. 00, and so on. Also, the above entails that the level of poverty in Zimbabwe has increased by 15 % since the colonial period, making majority of the Zimbabweans poorer than they were during the colonial era. What this entails is that even the levels of inequality have widened since the colonial period, with the gap between the poor and the rich widening accordingly. But what causes the differences in poverty levels within society?

Confronted by such a question, one is tempted to say it's laziness in some people and industriousness in others. Some would also suggest the differences in the status of families in which individuals are born. In fact, many others can be provided. I should, however, underscore that the underlying cause of differences in poverty levels in society is inequality. An inequality in resource distribution, for example, creates a gap between two people who have different access to the resource. This explains why poverty and inequality are normally considered as two sides of the same coin. They feed into each other such that we cannot separate inequality from poverty, the same way we cannot solve the egg-chicken problem. But what does it mean for Africa to say that poverty and inequality are opposite sides of the same coin?

Grossly in Africa, inequality is a creation of humanity though sometimes it is natural, biological or cultural. In many cases, inequality is created at planning level by the government, where poor planning cascades into inequality and ultimately impoverishment of others. I give an example of seed distribution which in Zimbabwe, due to political volatility, has been politicised such that it is distributed along partisan lines in the rural areas. The mere fact that one (person A) gets seed simply because s/he is deemed politically correct while the other (person B) is denied access to the seed on the grounds that s/he is deemed politically incorrect creates inequality between the two individuals. If A who got the seed manage to plant and have a successful (or bump) harvest and B who was denied access to the seed fails to secure it at all, the latter may be reduced to a pauper while the former becomes richer. This is how inequality breeds poverty. It is for such reasons that some critics argue that poverty in Africa is largely a creation of our own making, resulting from poor policies that cause uneven development among people. Where there is poor policy and planning at governmental level, people are bound to be poor whilst where there is good policy planning and sound policy, there is likely to exist even development. Thus, in short, it is arguably true that scenarios of inequalities are created through poor policies in areas like education, agriculture, language, credit facility, mining, and so on. But what creates the inequalities that in most cases cascade into poverty among others?

If inequalities are created, who (or what) create them? How are they perpetuated and sometimes internalised? I have already highlighted in the paragraph above that inequality is normally created at government level through policies, though even at community level inequalities, which are a replica of what is happening at governmental level, are inevitable. But besides policy, perception also results in inequalities. By perception, I mean how one views, understands, interpret and regards certain things. Perceptions normally come in different ways such as religion, ethnicity, ideology, and race (skin colour), among other such dimensions. Besides policy and perception, inequalities are also created by culture. Patriarchy in many societies such as those of Africa and Asia is a good example. In some societies such as the Moslem, women are for example not allowed to own properties such as land and houses. This was also the case in African societies such as Zimbabwe during colonialism and a few years after independence. Having said all this, we may need to critically examine how and when inequality in Africa generally started? Is it that pre-colonial Africa had high levels of inequality? Or, is it that inequality in Africa started during colonialism? Or broadly, is it that inequality is a new phenomenon in Africa?

The emergence of inequality in Africa

It is important to understand how the issues of inequality in Africa emerged. If we notice inequality in African societies, we need to trace when and how these started? Where there elements of inequality in the first societies or it can be thought of as a phenomenon that started as degeneration in African societies occurred, perhaps as a result of compound factors such as trade with the outer world, patriarch, and so on? If Africa degenerated into inequality at what point did this started? In effect, I am arguing that the earliest societies in Africa were egalitarian – where all human beings were equal. In other words, men and women in the egalitarian society were equal. This society was also highly mobile, moving from one place to another on seasonal basis. What was striking, however, were elements of different roles, for instance, egalitarian societies were hunter-gatherers. The concept "hunter-gather" was a collective reference term which shows that people were equal but with different roles based on sex and age. Men, for example, were hunters while women and children were gatherers. Wealth was communally owned, which means that issues of class were absent in the very earliest societies – the egalitarian. The human capital was the measure of wealth because this is where protection and security came from. Number – of women and children – determined the strength of society but without any hierarchical chain of command. While stratification was existent in a way, it existed particularly as some sort of organisation on behalf of the whole society and with no rewards attached to it, and had nothing to do with class.

As time went on, particularly during the stone age, the egalitarian society in Africa evolved itself due to the emergence of new skills – weaving, herbalism, iron smelting – amongst members of the society. It is common knowledge that skills, though can be taught, they cannot be shared, and so the emergence of new skills in the egalitarian society was a natural development. With the emergence of these new skills, it was no longer handy for egalitarian because people now wanted rewards for their extra skills i.e. for making arrows, beads, etc. This development also prompted barter trade between people both within the same society and with the external world. African societies, for example, started exchanging goods and services among themselves and with the outside world such as India and later China. It is worth noting that those who had the upper hand in this development were members of society with extra skills. These had more goods and services to exchange with others, making them distinct and richer than the rest. This marked the beginning of the first level of inequalities in the egalitarian society, prompting it to evolve for the first time from a classless society to a stratified society with distinct classes of people. I should therefore emphasise that the emergence of inequality in pre-colonial Africa was natural than it was artificial.

Moreover, the emergence of new skills saw the beginning of the domestication of animals and later the settling of people in one place – sedentary agriculture – as livestock accumulation – cattle, sheep, goats, donkeys etc. – increased. With the differences in skills, livestock accumulation which became one of the determinant measures of wealth and poverty amongst members of the same society, differed. Some members accumulated more livestock than others using their extra skills. Barter trading also became more effective and rewarding to people with extra skills. This heightened the levels of inequality in society with barter trade with the external world becoming even more rewarding both economically and socially.

With this realisation, more skills such as herbalism, weaving, iron smelting etc. increased giving more advantages to those with more talents and skills. Grain, artistic professions i.e. dancing, poetry, animals and the number of children and later crafting, started to be used as reference for wealth and poverty. This is when in African societies such as the Bantu Shona, terms like *mufumi* (rich person) and *murombo* (poor person) came into use. Visibility in society also became an issue, further heightening inequalities amongst members of the same society.

The Bantu migration which prompted people to identify arable land for permanent settlements which are the current settlements, perhaps marked the highest level of inequality ever in the pre-colonial African societies. In other words, the settling of people on permanent settlements brought in competition to accumulate more and more wealth for themselves, thereby marking the beginning of well pronounced inequality among members of the same society in the pre-colonial era.

I should note that domestication and farming using tools from iron smelting such as hoes reduced the intensity of hunting. Allocation of land started at household level thereby widening the inequalities. The different levels of production in the livestock side and grain production on the other side resulted in further inequality as people were moving from a classless society – egalitarian – to permanent settlements, with titles of skills such as hunters, weavers, spirit mediums, herbalists, weavers, wood curving, farmers/agriculturalists etc. The class of one's profession started to create class with professions such as agriculture (as it was more rewarding) given a higher status. Besides skills, gender also started to be seen as a determinant of class. Women and children began to be seen as members of the second and third class respectively after men – most of who were highly skilled. On marriage, particularly in the African patriarchal societies such as the Shona, Zulu, Tswana, Changani, Xhosa and others, women started to consider the skills and wealth that their would-be-husbands have. Those men deemed rich and highly skilled/talented had a competitive advantage such that they could marry the prettiest women in the society. Also, they would marry as many wives as they could. This made the number of wives and children a determinant of wealth and status in society as those men with many wives and children could cultivate larger pieces of land and automatically get more harvests than those with fewer wives and children. This was the state of affairs in many African societies at least up until the 1880s.

Around 1880s, we begin to see encroachment by missionaries in the African society. But one would wonder if the missionaries played any role in issues of inequality in Africa. The answer is a big YES! The missionaries extended or rather perpetuated gender inequality and as well as African patriarch through their religion – Western Christianity – where they preached that God created men and later his assistant, the woman. This teaching further reinforced the African philosophies that men are stronger (and therefore superior to women) and women are a weaker sex (and therefore inferior to men) and that for the same reason, women are for indoors activities while men are for the outdoors activities. A critical analysis of this teaching by the missionaries shows the major reason why Christianity did not get much resistance in the African societies that embraced patriarch such as the Shona, Ndebele, Zulu etc. On the contrary, the same teaching explains why missionaries had a torrid time penetrating matriarchal African societies such as the Tonga (Zimbabwe), the Herero (Namibia), and the Shwabo (Mozambique). Most of the Christian elements did not jig-saw fit in these African framework of matriarch as they fitted in the African framework of patriarch.

Thus during the missionary era and the scramble for Africa, the Western Marxist philosophy of life characterised by a patriarchal and vertical framework of life encroached in Africa. This had clear and visible classes. This system started by establishing industries following the employment of men in industrial zones – such as farming, factory and mining. Women were left idle in the rural areas for the major reason that the Western Marxist philosophy considered them a weaker sex. This philosophy therefore generally saw men being elevated to the potential to access resources as compared to their women counterparts, thereby widening the chasm between men and women in the African society. This was precipitated and further aggravated by the training and 'educating' of some men by the colonists in Africa. The training and level of education started even between men themselves with different classes determined by the level of education and training. In fact, three distinct classes of people were formed namely the skilled (the highly educated/trained), semi-skilled (the mediocrity), and the unskilled (the uneducated/untrained). In the industry, these classes of people, thus, were graded as such to the extent that their remunerations were pegged according to the grading system mentioned above. These three classes, thus, were unequal with levels of inequalities highly pronounced and indeed no longer a secret.

This period was followed by zonation which further classified Africa into zones. The industrial zone, for example, had the three classes discussed above –the skilled, semi-skilled and the unskilled. The industrial zone, thus, became the town with three distinct classes. These three different classes were also settled in different areas (or zones) namely the low density (for the skilled), medium density (for the semi-skilled) and the high-density (for the unskilled). For these three classes, salaries and other conditions of services were also gazetted accordingly.

The zonation system was not only effected in what is now called town. It was also effected in what is called rural areas today. In farming zones, land was divided in the same way with "whites" given large pieces of land simply because they were perceived as superior to their "black" counterparts. The European settlers were therefore put in the class of their own, with special treatment accorded to them by the colonial regime. The unproductive areas – sandy, unfertile and drought prone – were classified as Tribal Trust Land (TTL). These are the areas where all indigenous Africans were driven to live with their families. Even though the colonists knew that the soils in the TTL and rainfall pattern were poor to sustain human life, they forced the indigenous Africans to pay taxes to the colonial government to support the other zone – the commercial zone. This means that the people in the TTL were impoverished largely because of taxation and the areas they were forced to live in. This marked the end of egalitarianism in its totality in the African society with a few remnants prevailing in the TTLs. The same developments also marked the beginning of capitalism in Africa, creating classes of people with distinct rights and power.

I should underline that colonial education alongside capitalism further trained people to become more individualistic through certification. In fact, Western education was disastrous as far as creation and perpetuation of inequalities are concerned. It gave people different classes and professions with different grading and remuneration/salaries. Medicine and law, for example, were ranked higher professions than teaching, driving and others, thereby further perpetuating the class system and Western individualism in Africa. This has created distinct classes and inequalities even at household (family). For instance, two family individuals who are siblings are now distinguished and classified differently on the basis of their level of education and profession i.e. teacher and doctor with the latter ranked higher than the former.

Further, Western-biased governance hierarchy which is vertically hierarchical has been terribly worse in the history of inequality in Africa. African governance hierarchy was horizontal with everyone from the "royal" house considered a chief in some way and with the power to rebuke the chief who is representing them at family level. In fact chieftainship was not perceived as an individual thing or achievement but a family and community thing. European colonialism, which brought the vertical governance hierarch thus, widened classes and inequalities between people of the same society. The president, for example, through power has access to all resources. S/he is more equal than all others to the extent of being labelled as the first citizen if s/he is not the eldest citizen in the country.

I cannot afford to leave out globalisation and its role in perpetuating inequalities not only at national level but international level. Globalisation as initiated by the Global North has come to reinforce different societal values in countries of the Global South to ensure that the world is conceptualised as one system with similar laws yet the referee remains located in the Global North. This has driven further the idea of inequality now at the level of nations. This is compounded with the 21st century factors such as climate change, uneven distribution of resources (e.g. Somalia which is largely poor because there are no resources and this is coupled with war/conflict), uneven distribution of technology, war (or conflict), and uneven distribution of natural disaster (e.g. diseases, droughts, earthquakes, floods etc.) have all caused poor performance in some countries of the world making them more unequal and exploitable than others. Thus, basically this is how inequality in Africa has grown to reach the levels it has reached today.

The intricate relationship between poverty and inequality

In the section above shown how inequality, through its creation of classes in society, breeds poverty. What this means is that there is an intricate relationship between poverty and inequality. In fact, it should be noted that inequality and poverty go hand in glove. They can hardly be separated as they co-exist in a very complex way. Inequality in society can result in poverty while poverty can also result in poverty in some members of the society. In short, poverty and inequality overlap and feed into each other. The relationship between poverty can be represented by the diagram in fig. 1. below:

Fig. 1: Relationship between poverty and inequality

Where there are inequalities there is poverty somewhere somehow given that where there are inequalities we have classes of people, some classified as rich and others as poor. But what causes poverty? While causes of poverty particularly with reference to Africa are allegedly many ranging from inequality to individual deficiency, geographical location, colonialism, slave trade, diseases, natural hazards, poor governance, civil wars and unrest etc., I will look at the causes from a theoretical perspective. Thus, instead of looking at each of the mentioned factors in view of how it causes or perpetuate poverty, I will explain these using theories of poverty.

Theories of poverty

In the sections above, I introduced the concepts of poverty and inequality but you may still be wondering what actually causes poverty. In this section, I discuss the main theoretical explanations of poverty that have been discussed in literature. While theories of poverty could be many, in this book I underline that there are four major categories of theories of poverty. These are:

a). Individual deficiency theories

This category of theories explains poverty in terms of individual factors to argue that the individual is responsible for his/her poverty situation. In economic circles, poverty is associated with laziness and lack of creativity and innovation. Thus for those in the economic circles, some people are poor simply because they are either lazy to use their minds or to use their body to enrich themselves. This becomes a bit different when we shift to religion. In religious circles, poverty is associated with a curse or simply the absence of divine favour. In these circles, if one is cursed or lacks divine favour, s/he should seek divine favour through appeasement of the deity(-ies). Thus, generally speaking, individual deficiency theories argue that poverty can be avoided by either working harder or making better choices religiously or economically. According to these theories, some people are poor simply because they do not work hard enough or do lack incentives to improve their own conditions. In the science circles, other theories in this category explain poverty as a general lack of genetic and intelligent qualities to enrich themselves. In the education circles, more other theories in the same category explain poverty in terms of lack of well-planned goals and education as well as other requisite skills to enrich or improve oneself.

However, while these theories have received lots of attention in scholarship, they have been criticised by scholars such as Fischer, Hont, Kankowski, Lucas, Swidler and Voss (1996) for the major reason that they are being used as a lame excuse for social inequality in many societies. For these scholars, all inequalities are by design and never a result of natural differences such that there is need to demystify and even dislodge the individual deficiency theories.

b). Cycle of poverty theory

This category of theory explains poverty in terms of history of a people or individual. This theory, which is widely used in the field of economics, argues that a cycle of poverty is the set of factors or events by which poverty, once started, is likely to continue unless there is outside intervention. The cycle of poverty has been defined as a phenomenon where poor families become impoverished for at least three generations, i.e. for enough time that the family includes no surviving ancestors who possess and can transmit the intellectual, social, and cultural capital necessary to stay out of or change their impoverished condition (Marger 2008). As Valentine (1968) further explains, cycle of poverty occurs when poor people do not have the resources necessary to get out of poverty, such as financial capital, education, or connections. In other words, impoverished individuals do not have access to economic and social resources as a result of their poverty. This lack may increase the people's poverty situations very difficult to change such that poor people remain poor throughout their lives. Such poor people have either very limited or no resources at all, making it virtually impossible for individuals to break the cycle of poverty.

Another theory for the perpetual cycle of poverty is that poor people have their own culture – culture of poverty – with a different set of values and beliefs that keep them trapped within that cycle generation to generation. In fact, the culture of poverty theory explains poverty in terms of inherent structural deficiencies. For the theory, poverty is a creation of humanity because it results from the transmission over generations of a set of poor beliefs, values and skills that though individually held are socially generated. Such dysfunctional or maladaptive skills, beliefs and values are responsible for causing and perpetuating poverty in individuals, families and societies.

The culture of poverty theory has been explored by Ruby K. Payne (2005) in her infamous book: *A Framework for Understanding Poverty*, where she explains how a social class system in the United States of America exists, thereby creating a wealthy upper class, a middle class, and the working poor class. These classes each have their own set of rules and values, which differ from each other. To understand the culture of poverty, Payne describes how these rules affect the poor and tend to keep them trapped in this continual cycle. Time is treated differently by the poor; they generally do not plan ahead but simply live in the moment, which keeps them from saving money that could help their children escape poverty.

c). Economic and political distortions

This category of theories is an infusion of individual deficiency theory and culture of poverty theory. The theories in this category attribute poverty to the economic, political and social system, either of the past or of the present times, for causing people to have limited opportunities and resources to enrich themselves or to improve their situations (Bradshaw 2006). Theorists in this category, for instance, argue that the economic system in many societies is structured in such a way that poor people always fall behind regardless of their competences. Marx and Engels are two distinctive scholars who laboured to demonstrate that the economic system of capitalism strategically created a "reserve army of the unemployed" to ensure that wages are kept low.

Other theorists in this category explain poverty in terms of the inabilities or lack of opportunities for some to capitulate on the political system of their time. They argue, for example, that the poor are normally underrepresented or excluded in political discussions such that their interests are hardly catered for in the political process (Ibid).

d). Geographical disparities theory

Some scholars and researchers have now consistently shown that there is a relationship between poverty and distance from the economic growth centres. In fact for them, areas furthest from economic growth centres normally have the poorest households and individuals.

Besides, theorists in this category also believe that cultures, people and institutions in some areas lack appropriate resources needed to improve their situations. One theoretical approach within this broad theory namely, the economic agglomeration theory, for example, predicts that the existence of industry in an area attracts services and markets and ultimately investment. This creates conditions for affluence for the people in the geographical location concerned. Likewise, the existence of poverty as well as conditions leading to poverty such as low housing prices further generate more poverty as low housing prices in such areas further attracts more poor people leading to housing disinvestment by building owners (Ibid).

More other theorists in this category have also reasoned that limited flow of knowledge, skills and technology in the so-called backward or remote areas (the country-side) further frustrates any development efforts in the areas.

e). Zonation theory

Dualism theories, which have largely been applied in many developing countries as those of Africa, assume a split of economic and social structures of different sectors namely agriculture and industry, so that they differ in organisation, level of development, and goal structures. Usually, the concept of "economic dualism", differentiates between two sectors of economy:

i). The traditional subsistence sector consists of small-scale agriculture, handcraft and petty trade, has a high degree of labour intensity but low capital intensity and little division of labour, and;

ii). The modern sector of capital-intensive industry and plantation agriculture produces for the world market with a capital-intensive mode of production with a high division of labour.

These two sectors have little relation and interdependence and develop each according to its own pattern, which means that economically there are also differences between those working in either sectors. The modern sector can be considered as an economic enclave of industrial countries, and its multiplicator and growth effects will benefit the industrial countries but have little effect on the internal market.

What these two sectors imply, however, is that development in dualism concepts is the suppression of the other sector, in this case, the traditional sector by concentrating on and expanding the modern sector. Only with time, it is assumed, the trickle down effects will reduce and abolish dualism. In this line of thinking, the main problem is capital formation because its degree determines the scope and speed of expansion of the modern sector.

In general, agriculture has to provide the resources, labour as well as capital, for expanding the modern sector. In details, the strategies vary. Some theorists like Lewis, Fei and Ranis, assumed that a reduction of the labour force in the agriculture sector, because of the widespread disguised unemployment, would not reduce agricultural production. The productive employment of these labourers in the modern sector would increase the total production of the economy and hence priority of investment in industry is necessary. This has had an impact that in many countries, more focus has been given to the industrial sector thereby extending inequalities between people working in the two sectors.

It should be stressed that concentration on the modern sector led to an increasing regional disparity, rural urban migration, urban unemployment, a decrease in agricultural production, and hindrance in industrial development because of a lack of purchasing power in the rural areas. The anticipated trickle-down effects, as envisioned by dualist theorists, hardly ever happened. In practice, development plans following this line of thinking, instead, led to failures like the early Indian development planning. Therefore, other authors, like Jorgenson, Lele, and Mellor, emphasise the important role of agriculture at the beginning of development, preceding or parallel to industrial development in order to provide enough internal resources for the development process.

In Zimbabwe, the creation of zones at national level has not only extended inequalities but caused poverty in other people. For instance, there are some visible inequalities between the employed and unemployed, those working in the agriculture sector and those in the industrial sector, and those living in low density suburbs and those in the high density, hence a stratified society. For the first time in the history of Zimbabwe, such inequalities were created by the colonial government which created zones such as high density zones and low density zones, among many other forms of zonation. The reality that remains even today in the Zimbabwean society is the high inequality and poverty level existent between people who happen to be in different zones. Thus, one could argue that zonation has resulted in both poverty and inequality in societies such as those of Zimbabwe.

The persistence of poverty in developing countries: A look at Africa

Africa's poverty has largely been attributed to underutilisation of resources, among other reasons such as poor governance, corruption as well as neo-colonialism. It is for this reason that scholars like Alexander (2006) argues that the establishment of settler rule in Zimbabwe (as in many other parts of Africa) rested on violent dispossession that was predicated on the myth that the Africans were not able to sustainably use the natural resources at their disposal to improve their lot. This need to manage natural resources while "civilising" the people therein necessitated the need for the Global North, particularly Europe, to colonise Africa. Gil Scott-Heron confirmed this myth when he argued that, "First, white folks discovered Africa and claimed it fair and square. Cecil Rhodes couldn't have been robbing nobody 'cause he said there was nobody there,' thereby confirming the colonial settler myth that the African was not able to sustainably use his resources prior to the advent of colonialism. Such colonial settlers' perceptions of Africa influenced the geography of land dispossessions in Zimbabwe where they saw themselves as a burdened by a responsibility to administer '[...] both nature and natives in the tropics; [because] both were resources to be managed, improved, and developed for the benefit of metropole and colony" (Moore 2005: 13). It should, however, be underlined loud and clear that available evidence has shown beyond reasonable doubt that by the middle ages, many parts of Africa had already developed at equal (or even far greater) level than those of Europe (cf. Asante 1988, 1990, 2000; Rodney 1981; Mawere 2014d; Mawere and Mubaya 2016; Stoneman 1981). In fact, Africa of the time was not "poor", so to speak as the people enjoyed abundant resources which they exploited sustainably but at liberty. Besides, people lived collectively as a community upholding the African of Ubuntu/Unhu which emphasised the spirit of [unconditional] love and sharing among members of the society. Even those who "lacked" physical access to certain resources enjoyed those resources they lacked through other members of the society to the extent that lacking was rare as long as some members of the society had access to a resource. It is for this realisation that many scholars agree that poverty was rare if not non-existent in the per-colonial African societies.

Conclusion

This chapter has discussed the intricacy covering issues of poverty and inequality. It has been revealed that since time immemorial, poverty has remained at the centre stage of all the problems that have troubled Africa. Yet, one other major problem that have resiliently persisted and passed the test of time is inequality. Inequality and poverty have in many cases become understood as bed fellows or at least sides of the same coin. They have co-existed for too long and their relationship especially in view of Africa and many other world societies will certainly persist for many years to come. I have settled on this pessimistic conclusion owing to my observation that the enduring problems of poverty and food shortage as a result of population explosion, rising in cost of living, incremental despotic leadership in Africa, changing climatic conditions, yawning asymmetrical relationships between Africa and the international community, among other reasons, have over the years prompted many governments, scholars, researchers and theorists to seek permanent solutions that foster development in Africa and at a world scale, but in vain. The ground should be level at gender, national and international levels if poverty and inequality are to become history to the existential experience of the people of Africa and beyond.

Chapter 6

Development, Agriculture and the Diffusion of Technology in Rural Africa

"The knowledge that diffusion moves from an area of higher concentration to that of lower concentration seems to have deceived Western theorists of development to think that development will always move from the direction of the Global North to that of the Global South and never vice-versa or at least at equilibrium. This is, however, a proposition yet to be challenged if not discarded to the dustbin of oblivion" (Munyaradzi Mawere 2016).

Introduction

As captured in the quotation above, the scientific knowledge of diffusion that particles will always move from an area of higher concentration to that of lower concentration, has likely become the major influence of the North development theorists especially those who were involved in the agriculture revolution to think that if Africa is to develop, its development will always be inspired or initiated by the North. The question that remains unanswered even to date is: Why after decades of the success of agriculture revolution in countries like the United States of America and China, countries like Africa remain uninspired? In other words, if agriculture revolution elsewhere successfully took place in the 50s through the 70s, why the same revolution is yet to take place in Africa after all these years?

As I address this question, let me point out that agriculture, the world over, has witnessed a myriad of changes over the years in a bid to stimulate productivity growth and meet the demand for food by the world people. By agriculture, I mean the science and art of rearing animals and growing of crops for either subsistence or for commercial purposes. It should be noted, however, that the characteristic changes that agriculture has assumed over time though many and some with detrimental effects to the environment and human health, most if not all, were meant to improve productivity.

While agriculture before the Green Revolution in many world societies was largely characterised with subsistence and generally low productivity growth, the Green Revolution initiatives at a world scale, led by Norman Borlaugh – the Father of Green Revolution – saw great changes which made the latter to be credited for having saved over a billion people from starvation, through agricultural technological advancements and transfer from the Developed World to the Developing World. By technology, I mean the collection of skills, methods, processes and techniques embedded in machines, tools and devices used in the production of goods or services of value (Bain 1937; George and Scott 1980). The technological advancements that were exported from the Developed World to the Developing World through Green Revolution initiatives were characterised by the manufacturing and use of synthetic fertilisers. This has not only improved crop productivity growth, but also the quality of the yield thereof. As Ruttan (2002) notes, the intensive application of manufactured fertilisers, in the last half-century in many societies of the world resulted in advances in crop production.

Besides, the adoption of technology such as the expansion of irrigation infrastructure is one other characteristic of technological progress in agriculture that have made areas that formerly experienced low productivity growth to yield more than enough to feed the people. In Zimbabwe, for example, the area around Birchnough Bridge which is characteristically dry and in agro-region 4, has been made productive through canal irrigation using water from the Save River.

Advancements in technological and scientific knowledge is the other characteristic that has culminated into the production of high yields and improved crop varieties of cereal grains that mature early and are disease and drought resistant. In Zimbabwe, where maize is the most grown crop, such varieties include SC 401, SC 403, SC 407, SC 411, among others. As Hazell (2009) notes, such technological progress has not only witnessed high productivity, but also cheaper livestock as the latter also feed on fodder.

The adoption of 'modern' farm machinery such as tractors and combine harvesters, through mechanised farming, is another characteristic of technological progress that agriculture across the world has assumed in the past years. This has boosted both crop productivity and yield quality. Corroborating the same observation, FAO Director-General, Jose Graziano da Silva (2013) has noted with reference to China that "China's agricultural production has been tremendously successful. Since 1978, the volume of agricultural production has grown almost five fold and the country has made significant progress towards food security." It should be underlined that the success of China has largely been a result of its embracing of mechanised farming and growing of high yielding crops such as rice and wheat besides its liberal economic policies.

More so, high yield varieties of common staple grains such as maize, rice, corn and wheat that were introduced in many parts of the world as a part of the green revolution initiatives qualifies as a characteristic of technological progress in agriculture. This characteristic of technological progress in agriculture has witnessed increased global crop productivity since the later part of the 20th century when due to technological advancements in agriculture. No wonder OECD- FAO (2013) has shown that global agricultural production is growing steadily at a rate of more than 1.5% a year on average, with this rate expected to be maintained over the coming decade.

Further, the use of crop protection chemicals such as herbicides and insecticides is yet another characteristic of technological progress in agriculture that has improved crop productivity growth over the years. As Tilman *et al* (2002) observe, it takes a decade or two for herbicide-resistant weeds to emerge and for insects become resistant to insecticides within about a decade. This gives farmers time to increase crop productivity.

Also, modernisation of management techniques, distribution of hybridised seeds as well as crop rotation, are other characteristics of technological progress exported to agriculture through Green Revolution initiatives, with the objective of improving agricultural productivity growth. In fact, with these new characteristics of technological progress in agriculture, the crop rotation substituted monocultures that were previously used yet they increased the number of pests, which compromised both the quantity and quality of the yield.

With all the characteristics of technological progress in the area of agriculture discussed in this chapter, recent studies by OECD-FAO (2013) have shown that global agricultural production is expected to grow steadily at a rate of 1.5% a year on average over the coming decade. As OECD-FAO, further note, the growth was expected to be even higher than this had not been the global rising production costs, price volatility, recurring droughts, growing resource constraints and increasing environmental pressures in the recent years. The grand question, however, is whether this growth would be as steadily high as 1.5 % in Africa as it could be in the so-called developed countries.

The determinants of the rates of diffusion of technical change in agriculture

The rate at which technical change in agriculture has occurred varies from place to place and from time to time depending on the circumstances of the area in question. This section critically discusses the determinants of the rates of diffusion of technical change in agriculture such as population growth, recurring droughts, erratic rainfalls, migration, and education literacy, among others.

To start with, agriculture is generally the rearing of animals and growing of crops for either subsistence or commercial purposes. Some scholars like Balter (2013) argue that the earliest development in agriculture dates back to around 13,000 years ago in the Near East around Chogha Golan in modern-day Iran where wild barley, wheat and lentils were cultivated. Others argue that agriculture arose in the Fertile Crescent near the Mediterranean – modern-day Israel,

Palestine, Syria, Jordan and Turkey) and spread across the world from there (cf. Riehl *et al* 2013). More others argue for "the multiple origins of agriculture" furthering that agriculture began independently and naturally in both the Old World (for example, Africa and the Middle East) and the New World (for example, America), a view that is gaining credence due to continued findings in early farming sites (see Larson *et al* (2014). Whatever the case, it is evident that hunter-gatherers first began to domesticate wild animals (such as wild goats) and gather and plant seeds from wild cereals and legumes such as barley, lentils and barley for their own subsistence, as early as 13,000 years. Their agriculture, characteristically in the form of shifting cultivation and pastoralism in general, required less advanced tools such that production was relatively low and mainly for subsistence.

Due to a rise in population, the demand for more food also increased causing some scholars such as Thomas Malthus to predict that by the turn of the twenty-first millennium, the earth would not be able to support its growing population. The prediction, however, turned otherwise due technological change in agriculture that has allowed the world to produce even surplus food (Alexei and Keith 2005). Though Malthus' prediction turned otherwise due to, "necessity *which* is the mother of invention" (Plato in the Republic), population growth demanded the invention of new ways of improving agriculture productivity to avoid disasters such as death from hunger. Population growth prompted the birth of Green Revolution. Green Revolution refers to a series of research, development and technology transfer initiatives that occurred at a world scale between the 1930s and late 1970s, with the effect that it increased agriculture production around the world (Hazell 2009). The term "Green Revolution" was first used in 1968 by the former United State Agency for International Development (USAID) director, William Gaud, after noting the alarming spread of the new technologies. Gaud, thus, notes: "These [new technologies] and other developments in the field of agriculture contain the makings of a new revolution. It is not a violent Red Revolution like that of the Soviets, nor is it a White Revolution like that of the Shah of Iran. I call it 'the

Green Revolution" (Gaud 8 March 1968). Due to population explosion in Mexico, one of the most populated countries in the world, Green Revolution through irrigation technology and high yield crops (wheat and maize) occurred between 1950 – 1970, with the support of the United States government, United Nations, Food and Agriculture Organisation (FAO) and the Rockefeller Foundation. This concerted effort which led to the establishment of the International Maize and Wheat Improvement Centre (CIMMYT) – an international agricultural research centre – in 1943 by the Mexican government, significantly solved Mexico's problem of lack of food self-sufficiency by increasing crop productivity (Barkin 1997; Cotter 2003). As Jacobsen (2014: 4) observes:

> Important technologies that are essential for civilisations to take off are agriculture, iron working and writing. Agriculture needs to be at a certain level so there is a surplus in society and some of the population can take on other tasks than producing food, such as skilled labour, cultural functions and bureaucratic functions. Iron working is essential since iron is much stronger, cheaper and more durable than copper or bronze. Iron makes farming, industry and warfare more efficient and is therefore very important in a historical perspective. Both agriculture and ironworking have been present in sub-Saharan Africa and around the same time it emerged in other regions.

Yet, this is not to say that Green Revolution at the level of Africa started in the 1930s. In fact, the practice of "Green Revolution" outdates the coinage and usage of the term in literature. It is believed that the Bantu people from north-west Africa with iron smelting, crop cultivation and animal rearing knowledge pollinated their agricultural knowledge to the Khoisan people of Southern Africa. In fact, the Beba people who lived around the Sahara Desert and were largely raiders as well as pastoralists, started moving into the areas of the Bantu people as a result of worsening climatic conditions around the desert (Shillington 2002; 2012). This prompted the Bantu people to move southwards in search of new pastures and land, thereby spreading their technological and practical knowledge of agriculture to the Khoisan people of the south. This means that migration, just like population explosion, has been another determinant that played a significant role in the diffusion of technical change in agriculture.

With the increasing poverty levels and recurring droughts in Africa, investing in agriculture has also been seen as the only surest way to reduce poverty and hunger. With this realisation, the Alliance for a Green Revolution in Africa (AGRA) was formed in 2006 on the belief that investing in agriculture would rescue the majority of Africans languishing in poverty and hunger. Having been inspired by the former United Nations Secretary-General, Kofi Annan's call for a uniquely African "green revolution" to improve smallholder farm productivity while preserving the environment, AGRA has since supported in various more than 400 projects across the continent such as developing and delivering high yielding and drought resistant seed, improve soil fertility, upgrade storage facilities, improve market information systems, strengthen farmers associations, encourage environmentally friendly farming methods, expand access to credit to farmers and, advocate for national policies that benefit smallholder farmers (AGRA 2012). Such an initiative by AGRA, thus has, in a bid to improve food security, sped up the rate of diffusion of technical change in agriculture across the continent's rural areas which make up 70 % of Arica's population.

The improvement in agricultural knowledge in many societies across the globe has also become a determinant factor to speed up technological changes in agriculture. In the 1960s in the Republic of the Philippines, for example, the government with the help of Ford Foundation and the Rockefeller Foundation, established an International Rice Research Institute (IRRI), which resulted in the production of new rice varieties. The varieties, generally known as the IR8 produced substantially higher yields than traditional cultivars leading to an annual increase of rice production to rise from 3. 7 million tons to 7. 7 million tons in two decades since the 1996 breeding lines of IR8 initiative (Cotter 2003).

Famine is another determinant of the rates of diffusion of technical change in agriculture. In 1961, India was on the brink of mass famine. In the Indian sub-continent countries, famine had been recurrent such that there are 14 recorded famines (such as the Bengal Famine of 1770 and 1943, the Damajipant Famine, the Great Famine of 1876-78, the Deccan Famine, and the Gujarat Famine which claimed 3 million people) between the 11th and 17th centuries as well as more than 60 million deaths recorded between the 18th and 20th centuries: the last major famine was the Bengal Famine of 1943 (Lancaster 2000; Mehta 2001). The Damajipant Famine is recorded to have caused serious several deaths of both people and animals in the northern and southern parts of India (Attwood 2005). In response to these series of famines, the Indian government had to hire the services of American agronomist and father of Green Revolution, Norman Borlaugh to allow the diffusion of agricultural technological expertise from the Developed World to India (Indian Express 1950). With the assistance of Ford and Rockefeller Foundations, India embarked on a Green Revolution programme of plant breeding, irrigation development, and financing agrochemicals to overcome chronic food defects. The programme, which started in the 1960s successfully increased India's food productivity growth and security.

Conclusion

As a matter of conclusion, one should be reminded that the determinants for the diffusion of technological change in agriculture are many, ranging from social, political, economic and necessity. Besides, determinants for the diffusion of technological change in agriculture differ circumstantially from place to place. In this chapter, I have highlighted and meticulously explained with reference to recorded cases and examples, how determinants such as famine, improved agricultural knowledge, increased poverty levels, population explosion and migration of people at different times of human history have propelled the diffusion of technological change in agriculture across the world.

Chapter 7

Gender and Development in Africa

"A fire fighter who fights smoke will never extinguish the fire up until a point he realises it is the fire that he needs to fight" (Munyaradzi Mawere 2016).

Introduction

For a long, development pathways especially in Africa have experimented on many things – policies, strategies, theories, models and frameworks – without identifying the core of what really needs to be done in order to develop the continent. Gender discourse, especially gender mainstreaming is one among many other ingredients of development that has been lacking for many years now on the continent. Africans, thus, have been like fire fighters fighting smoke when they wanted to extinguish fire.

The evolution of gender and development thinking, policies and current trends in Africa could be understood best if looked at from a historical perspective. In Africa, as elsewhere in the Western world, development initiatives and theorisation in the past ignored the role and position of women in the whole matrix of development. In the early decades after the second World War, for example, the modernisation theories of the time perceived developed as a linear process of change where traditional societies (as those of Africa, Latin America, Asia etc.) would evolve from their tradition-bound "backwardness" to [Western] modernity through adoption of the Western technologies, values and institutions. Through further theorisation and most especially since the 1975 United Nations Conference on women in Nairobi, Kenya, the need to incorporate women in the matrix of development has not only been perceived as a necessity but an indispensable move. The relevance of gender and various attempts at improving the condition of women in society have remained topical. This chapter explore the different perspectives at both global and continental levels that have (and continue) to be refined in view of the position ad role of women in development.

Problematising gender

It is sometimes very difficult to understand exactly what is meant by the term "gender," especially how it differs from the closely related term "sex". Let us make it clear here that "sex" simply refers to the biological and physiological characteristics that define men and women. On the other hand, "gender" refers to the socially constructed roles, behaviours, activities and attributes that a given society consider appropriate for men and women respectively. Gender is normally categorised as feminine and masculine while "sex" is categorised as female and male. What we make of this is that gender is a social construction while sex is a physiological characteristic of humanity. The problem, however, is that the moment we accept that gender is a social construction, we would want to understand why some issues were or are constructed as such. And even so, we would want to know if the way some issues were socially constructed in the past is the best one such that it remains unchallenged.

Why gender for development?

As Khosla *et al* (2004) tell us, there is considerable evidence that a gender-sensitive approach to development leads to greater efficiency, effectiveness, equality and equity. What this means is that a combined effort and recognition of the importance of both men and women in all development endeavours translate to a more habitable society that is better off in wholesomely improving the condition of humanity. This thinking resonates with that of Connelly *et al* (2000) who argue that the concern with gender relations in development has gone a long way in affirming the idea that equality in the status of men and women is fundamental to every human society if that society is to realise development.

It is such kind of fair thinking that, over the past three decades, has witnessed the refinement of development perspectives particularly on what "true" development could be and how it can be brought about more effectively and efficiently. This refinement has fortunately opened opportunities for both men and women to earn sustainable livelihoods while creating conducive environments for all. It has also afforded equal voices to both men and women in decision making, policy making and implementation, and in governance. In the next section, I focus on the contemporary frameworks of development that have been adopted over the years in a bid to achieve equality and equity in issues of development.

Contemporary frameworks of development

a). Women in development (WID)

In 1975, the United Nations, through a Conference in the Mexico City, launched 'a decade for women' under the theme "equity, development and peace." The main goal of the Conference and indeed for launching a decade for women was to integrate women into the process of development (cf. Moser 1993). Women, thus, were integrated in development; what has come to be known as women in development (WID). This prompted many governments around the world to set offices for women's affairs to address the problems and needs of women in society. The main goal of WID was to increase efficiency in production and service provision (Meena 1992). Unfortunately, the WID implementers along with their donor agencies continued to work within the paradigm of modernisation where adoption of Western technology, institutions and values was believed to be the yardstick to measure development: WID assumed that Western institutions had all the answers to gender issues and problems, thereby ignoring the possible contribution of knowledge systems. WID approach, in fact, tended to concentrate on the role of women as producers and ignored their domestic roles as labourers in the home. In this regard, WID generally ignored the impact of women subordination, global inequalities on women in the developing world as well as the importance of race and class in women's lives. To achieve development, the theorists and planners of development projects believed that women should be added into the development matrix by opening up opportunities for them in areas of education, training, property ownership, employment and credit facilities. Also, the theorists for WID argued that women must be integrated into development projects in such a way that they are afforded a voice in policy design and implementation. Thus for these theorists, until women are included at all these levels development policies would continue undermining women's status in society. However, as highlighted above, WID strategies in many developing countries such as those of Africa did not provide an alternative from the modernist approach to development. As Meena (1992) argues, "WID led to an increase of donor-funded income generating activities for women, but these activities were not part of the mainstream plans" (p. 20). For this reason, women who in fact were supposed to be the main actors at the centre stage of development found themselves at the margins as marginal actors in planning, implementing, monitoring and evaluating development projects. Consequently, the WID strategy did not improve the status of women besides failing to build their self-esteem and enhance their capacities to get involved in development planning and execution (cf. Mbilinyi 1992). These problems associated with WID led critical scholars such as Mbilinyi (Ibid) to summarise the limitations of WID strategy as follows:

- WID experts assumed that they knew best the strategies and objectives the poor women of the developing world should adopt to move out of their poverty box. The experts thus never bothered to observe, learn from, and listen to the "suffering" women themselves;
- WID strategy left out men, yet men are part and parcel of the story of gender relations in any society;

- WID strategy added more work onto the women's shoulders without alleviating their other responsibilities in production;
- WID strategy neither questioned the nature of development itself at local, national and international levels nor the existing international division of labour; and
- WID strategy viewed women as simple victims rather than as potential allies in coalitions built by different groups of women at all levels from the local to international.

b). Women and development (WAD)

In the late 1970s, shortfalls of the WID perspective were noted. In particular, it was noted that women were already integrated into the development processes of the society, but this integration was unfair and deserved justice for it to be effective. This led to campaigns for a Women and Development (WAD) perspective, which in itself was meant to cater for the omissions in WID. With WAD, proponents of the perspective argued that development projects should always increase access the access of women to resources, decision making and power positions taking into account their the demands and roles they already play in society.

From the above, it can be noted that WAD argued for the recognition of the distinctiveness of position in society, their knowledge, responsibilities and goals. For WAD proponents, failure to recognise this distinctiveness of women, particularly the special role they have always played in development in their respective communities as happened with the WID perspective, will never free them from their previous disadvantages. Neither would that failure promote the progression of women from their present position.

As such, for WAD proponents, there was need to change national and global development policies to ensure that the omissions in the WID perspective are properly addressed. Besides, the proponents highlighted the need to disseminate information to all stakeholders, especially women themselves, in the development process was key to strengthening ties among women and their network groups, as well as ensuring the emancipation and progression of women in society.

It is important, however, to note that while WAD tried to offer important corrective measures to improve the WID perspective, it equally had weaknesses and less-attentive assumptions. In fact, while WAD managed to correct the assumption that challenging male-dominated states would alter gender inequalities, it also readily and generally assumed that solutions to problems affecting all women of the world can be found in the close examination of experiences and problems of particular groups of women. Such an assumption was dangerous given that experiences and problems of women vary from group to group or society to society. In fact, even among women in the same society, experiences and problems may vary. Such realisations made many feminists and development theorists to be critical of both WID and WAD as they perceived that none of them addressed the fundamental gender gaps and inequalities in society. This resulted in campaigns for a third perspective known as Gender and Development (GAD).

c). Gender and development (GAD)

As noted above, the inadequacies in both WID and WAD resulted in the campaigns for a new perspective, Gender and Development (GAD). Unlike WID and WAD which emphasise that women should be part and parcel of all development processes in the community, GAD, which began in the early 1980s and launched officially in the 1985 Nairobi International Non-Governmental Organisation Forum, recognises that it is not only women that are disadvantaged, but also poor men and other less fortunate groups such as the visually challenged, the mentally retarded, and the physically challenged. This means that for GAD, women, less fortunate groups and poor men remain the victims of social structures in many communities. Thus, for GAD it is not only women that need to be elevated in society, but what is most appropriate is that men and women work together for purposes of development and improvement of society as a whole. In this working together, GAD proposes that both men and women must seek to understand the different development priorities as well as needs of all people and make sure that they are fully involved in decision making on issues that affect them at all levels as a society. It is from this understanding of this new perspective that Sen and Grown (1987) to note that GAD recognises the importance of gender and global inequalities. GAD's main points of emphasis can be summarised as follow:

- Gender is not only a women's issue but a societal issue;
- Women tend to be disadvantaged in society as compared to their male counterparts;
- Less fortunate groups are also disadvantaged in society as compared to men;
- Men and women have different and special needs that should be equally respected;
- Gender issues if not properly managed can also result in men being disadvantaged;
- Inequalities in society are often structural and systematic;
- Women though generally tend to be disadvantaged cannot be treated as a homogeneous group.

It should be underscored that GAD emerged mainly from the writings and grass-roots organisational researches and experiences of feminist activists in developing countries through their organisational group known as Development Alternatives with Women for a New Era (DAWN), besides the experiences and analysis of Western socialist feminists interested in development issues (Moser 1989). It should be underlined that drawing on a socialist-feminist perspective, the GAD perspective argues that the position of women in national, regional and global economies as well as their material conditions of life and patriarchal power deeply affect the their status in society (Sen and Grown 1987). In addition to this, Sen and Grown, would further argue in view of the GAD perspective that patriarchal authority and women's material conditions are both defined and perpetuated by the accepted societal norms and values that define women and men's duties, roles and position in their respective societies. Thus, GAD perspective focuses more on the relationship between gender, race, culture, colonial history, class, position in economic order, and the social constructions that arises as a result of all these tugs.

Recently, GAD has however been criticised for being sectorial and project specific instead of being holistic to cater for both sexes' interests in a manner that ensure equitable and sustainable development at all levels of the society.

d). Gender Mainstreaming (GM)

Basing on the criticism of GAD highlighted above, another perspective has been postulated. This perspective is Gender Mainstreaming (GM). As the United Nations Economic and Social Council (1997) notes, GM is a strategy for making women's as well as men's concerns and experiences an integral dimension of the policies and programmes in all political, economic, and societal spheres so that men and women benefit equally and inequality is not perpetuated. It recognises that where there is need to promote the elevation of a particular sex (whether male, female or otherwise), it has to be necessarily done as such. This means that the GM perspective incorporate the GAD perspective in its programmes. It's only that GM's main objective is to comprehensively look at the relationship between men and women in terms of their access and control over resources, benefits and rewards, and decision making at all levels of the society, be it an institution, organisation, government or the entire society. What this mean is GM emphasises that both men and women should have equitable access to resources, rewards, participation, and opportunities, with favour or segregation based on lines of gender. It implies that becoming part of the GM offers the society an opportunity for equal participation, influence what has to be done in society and by who, who should own what, who should (and can) have access to what (including jobs, income, and other such resources), who should (and can) control and manage the society's resources, priorities, and institutions as well as who should determine the society's goals and destiny.

With its emphasis on equality between different sexes, GM has gained global support and influence as it is now often used as the foothold for promoting gender equality. One of the merits of the GM perspective is that it promotes generative dialogue amongst society members in all areas ranging from resource allocation, legislation, policy development, research, project planning, designing, implementation, monitoring and evaluation. What we make of this is that gender mainstreaming is a fundamental aspect of good governance: it advocates equity, equality and the promotion of human rights in general. It ensures that policies, institutions and programmes at all levels respond to the needs and interests of both men and women in society. As such, with its emphasis on equity, justice, fairness, and democratic processes, gender mainstreaming is said to contribute immensely to the economic, social, cultural, and political progress of society. Gender mainstreaming's main points of emphasis can be summarised as follow:

- It is a long-term, transformative process that seriously reconsider the society's policies, cultural norms and values, programmes and goals;
- It is a long-term process that involves changing institutions, policies and programmes in a way that promote gender equity, fairness and equality;
- It is a development strategy that is used to work towards the fulfilment of gender equality without making it an end in itself;
- It is a democratic governance approach that ensures that both men and women's concerns and experiences are equally considered when planning, designing, implementing, monitoring and evaluating development projects at all levels;
- It is a long-term development strategy that seeks to level the ground for all societal members regardless of their sex, orientations, race, education or class.

However, I should be quick to point out that gender mainstreaming has, just like all its predecessors, has met with criticism. The United Nations Development Programme, for example, has noted in its reviews that although of good intentions, gender mainstreaming still have a long way to go in terms of delivering all its promises in areas of allocation of resources, accountability in gender equality issues, translation of commitment into action, implementation and enforcement, and will, among others.

Conclusion

As has been noted in the discussion in this chapter, gender issues are pertinent in the area of development. It has been made clear that gender equity, fairness, and justice are critical in fostering and steering development at all levels of the society. However, has been evidenced in the different perspectives postulated over time, it has never been easy to reach a consensus on which perspective can really sustain development in a manner that is universally acceptable. The gender mainstreaming perspective, which seem to have been widely accepted has, for example, also met with criticism. The major criticisms of the gender mainstreaming perspective were clearly outlined in the Beijing Declaration of 1997. In this declaration (cited in Gwekwerere 2000), six critical areas of concern that all the perspectives – WID, WAD, GAD, and MD –, still fall short of are:

- Gender capacity building;
- Lack of respect for, and inadequate promotion and protection of human rights of women and the girl child;
- The situation of women in the context of armed and political conflict;
- The inequalities in economic structures and policies in economic productive activities at all levels of society;
- Insufficient mechanisms to promote women advancement at all levels of society.

Thus, although several perspectives of gender and development have been postulated in a bid to achieve what one would consider as sustainable development built on the democratic principles of equity, equality, fairness and justice, none of these perspectives has so far managed to do justice to society, particularly women, as they engage in the processes of development. In view of this understanding, there is no doubt that yet another perspective should be launched once again. However, emphasis should be made on the need for thoughtfulness, cogency, and pragmatism on the launching of this perspective as the idea is not only about launching perspectives for launching purposes, but to launch perspectives that are critical to the promotion of sustainable development that underline development justice principles of equity, equality, and fairness.

Chapter 8

Social Policy and Development in Africa

An enduring chock-full framework tempo of development can only derive its roots in a sound social policy (Munyaradzi Mawere 2016).

Introduction

As reflected in the quotation above, a sound development framework for any country can only derive its roots from a comprehensive social policy. A comprehensive social policy comes from the people, for the people and with people at the centre. It should be people driven. Two important questions arise: Could underdevelopment in Africa a result of social policies that do not come from the people? If Africa's policies are people driven, why then the continent is failing to develop an enduring chock-full framework tempo of development for its adoption?

As we reflect on these questions and many others to be raised herein, it is worthwhile to note that Africa is a continent with mixed histories, some that are interesting and others sad. These histories, especially the sad ones, have in most cases been implicated in the discourses on Africa's underdevelopment and other such challenges that haunt the continent. Having noted development challenges associated with the continent, African governments, through the African Union (AU) and Southern African Development Cooperation (SADC), have put their heads together to come up with the Social Policy for Africa. The policy was meant to guide and steer development while trying to avoid the mistakes and misfortunes of the past.

Some more questions that remain lingering and even boggling are: With all the development policies in place why Africa remains poor or even poorer than yesterday? Is it because Africa's policies are foreign to its own context? Is it because Africa simply adopts policies from other continents such as Europe and America without a proper sense of how to implement them? Or is it because Africa is good at setting standards it can never be able to achieve? It is in view of all these questions that in this chapter, I seek to make a critical appraisal of the African framework of social policy in view of development efforts (or lack of it) by African governments. On this note, social policy will be examined chiefly with reference to AU and SADC efforts to improve human condition on the continent.

Understanding policy

The term policy is not only complex but dynamic in so far as it encompasses a whole range of aspects. This makes the term "policy" very challenging for many people to define with precision. As such, the term "policy" has enjoyed a wide array of definitions. Dodd and Boyd (2000), for example, define policy as a plan of action agreed upon by a group of people with the power to carry it out as well as effect it. This understanding makes it clear that policy acts in a given environment, hence its making is conditioned and shaped by social, historical, political and economic as well as many other such factors.

As has been highlighted above, policy encompasses a number of aspects. The realisation that policy encompasses a lot of aspects has prompted scholars like Cunningham (1963) to liken policy to an elephant which one knows when s/he sees it yet defining it is difficult (see Keeley and Scoones 1993). In this book, policy shall be understood as a guiding principle adopted by a group of people, organisation, state or any other such entity to help its operations. This understanding of policy lays bare the following major points:

i). That policy making and adoption is deliberate;
ii). That policy guides human action and decision making;
iii). That policy is intentional or purposive/goal oriented: it seeks to achieve desired outcomes/goals;
iv). That policy is action focused: it spells out clearly what is to be done, how, by who and for whom to be done.

Having said all this, one still wonders what we mean by a social policy. For Kabeer and Cook (2000), social policy is a mechanism that allows for government collective-led interventions to be adopted and implemented to protect or improve the lives of citizens by the government. Generally speaking, a social policy (also known in public policy) encompasses all guiding frameworks for public provision by the government. This means that social policy is multidimensional in so far as it seldom encompasses a single action, but often a series of actions coordinated to achieve a goal. Goals to be achieved normally fall within the public realm including areas normally intervened by the government such as education, health, public welfare, sport, culture, human rights, animal rights, transport, social security, justice, child welfare, housing and many others. This, in a nutshell, means that social policy seeks to achieve a desired goal that is generally considered to be in the best interest of all members of the society concerned by making a rational choice so as to ensure maximum social gain. When applied to social policy, maximum social gain dictates that the government should always "choose policies which result in gains to society which exceed costs by the greatest amount, and government should refrain if costs are not exceeded by gains" (Dye 1987: 30).

Africa's framework of social policy

To begin with, African framework of social policy is a continental binding document stating the vision and mission of the continent. As a policy document, it spells out the guiding principles to be followed by all African governments. Owing to the complexities and polysemousness of policy as a concept, the proliferation of literature policy (and social policy) debate has been a never ending process since the inception of the concept, such that these concepts have enjoyed different interpretations through time. In this essay, policy shall mean a deliberate basic course or principle of action that guides an individual, government, or an organisation, in this case, AU

(Office of General Council, 2012), while by social policy, we mean a mechanism that allows for collective state-led measures implemented by the state and its partners – the private sector, civil society and international development partners – to protect vulnerable groups, by guaranteeing basic economic and social conditions, overcoming structural deficiencies in the distribution of wealth and productive assets, creating greater equality for all, and rectifying market failure (Kabeer and Cook, 2000). In other words, social policy is what the government decides to do (or not to do) – the actions or inactions of a government (Dye 2000). Overall, a social policy must be concerned with public provisions by the government to ensure three things: economic growth, particularly the redistributive effects of economic policy; social protection – protect people from the vagaries of the market and the changing circumstances of age, illness and disability, enhance the productive potential of members of society; and to reconcile the burden of reproduction with that of other social tasks (cf. Mkandawire 2004). Thus, a social policy is people-centred concerned with collective public efforts aimed at protecting and improving social wellbeing: it has people as the drivers and the beneficiaries of sustainable development. The African framework of social policy was incubated at the first session of the African Union (formerly Organisation of African Unity [OAU]) Labour and Social Affairs Commission (AUC) held in Mauritius in 2003, with a follow-up [1st] session of the AU Conference of Ministers in charge of social development held in Namibia in 2008. The Ministers present during the 2003 Commission recommended and requested that the Commission in consultation with stakeholders, should develop a Social Policy Framework for Africa (SPF) to compliment as well as supplement the ongoing national and regional programme and policy initiatives meant for socio-economic integration and development such as the Poverty Reduction Strategy (PRSP), the 1980 Lagos Plan of Action (LPA), the 1994 Abuja Treaty, and the 2001 New Partnership for African Development (NEPAD) as well as to close the gap where it perceived these did not adequately address social issues. It was spelt out during the Commission that "the vision and mission of the African Union Commission (AUC) is to build an integrated, prosperous and peaceful Africa, using the best of the continent's human and material resources" (AU Conference of Ministers 2008: 4). As a continental social policy framework, the SPF for Africa was meant to enhance the attainment of the AU Social Affairs Department's ambition of promoting:

A holistic and human-centred approach to socio-economic development, and intra-and inter-sectorial coordination of the social sector with a view to alleviating poverty and improving the quality of life of the African people, in particular the most vulnerable and marginalised.

As such, the SPF focuses, in no particular priority, on 18 key thematic social issues that affect and impact on the people of Africa in many different ways namely: population and development; labour and employment; Social Protection, health; HIV/AIDS, TB, malaria and other infectious diseases; migration; education; agriculture, food and nutrition; the family; children, adolescents and youth; ageing; disability; gender equality and women's empowerment; culture; urban development; environmental sustainability; the impact of globalisation and trade liberalisation in Africa; good governance and anti-corruption and; Rule of Law (AU Conference for Ministers 2008). Besides these 18 areas, four other issues were identified as also deserving critical and immediate attention in Africa. These are: drug and substance abuse and crime prevention; sport; civil strife and conflict situations; and foreign debt. The AUC programme on social development, thus, is based on a people-centred approach that has, as its core value, the aspiration to promote human dignity, rights and desirable life. The need for a Social Policy Framework for Africa was, in fact, necessitated by the African Union's vision to "build an integrated, prosperous and peaceful Africa, an Africa driven and managed by its own citizens and representing a dynamic force in the international arena" and, to achieve by 2025:

> A united and integrated Africa; an Africa imbued with the ideals of justice and peace; an inter-dependent and virile Africa

determined to map for itself an ambitious strategy; an Africa underpinned by political, economic, social and cultural integration which would restore to Pan-Africanism its full meaning; an Africa able to make the best of its human and material resources, and keen to ensure the progress and prosperity of its citizens by taking advantage of the opportunities offered by a globalised world; an Africa engaged in promoting its values in a world rich in its disparities.

The grand mind boggling questions now is: Will Africa, through its African framework of social policy, achieve all its intended goals by 2025? Or, what has SPF for Africa done (or not done) so far to achieve development on the continent? Or to what extent is SPF helping Africa to reverse the legacy of colonialism, exploitation, and abject poverty, in its many countries? All these questions though different in semantics demand the same answer, particularly on what has Africa achieved (or not achieved) in view of its 2003 SPF.

In view of this question, it can be noted that there are some teething challenges confronting the framework of social policy in Africa. It is these challenges that have witnessed aggravating poverty levels, debilitating and falling standards in health care service provision and standard of living, economic smelting and other such problems in many African countries. It is also in light of these challenges that the AU Conference of Ministers (2008: np), envisaged that the aspiration to promote human dignity, rights and desirable life is likely to be held back unless the ominous social developmental problems facing the continent such "as a high burden of disease, lack of basic infrastructure, and social services, inadequate health care and services; poor access to basic education and training; high illiteracy rates; gender inequality; youth marginalisation; and political instability in a number of countries" is adequately attended to. This observation by the AU Conference of Ministers was drawn from the major characteristic of many African countries, that the condition of the ordinary people in the continent has remained the same or worse than during colonialism. In fact, though various policy reforms were introduced and implemented to mitigate the different socio-economic problems experienced by African countries and to reduce poverty, Africa has remained poor or even poorer than before. A majority of the African countries, for example, initiated and carried out substantial policy transformations during the 1986-1990 period; policies which have emphasised rationalisation and liberalisation of prices, especially exchange rates, food price structures and interest rates, prioritisation of public expenditure towards human investment and infrastructure, access to economic and political participation, reduction of absolute poverty, and where practicable, reduction of military expenditure (see UN General Assembly Report 1991). Such policy reforms, which in many cases, started with Structural Adjustment Programmes (SAPs) of the 1980s, which were designed by Bretton Woods Institutions (the World Bank and the International Monetary Fund) for the purpose of bringing about economic growth and recovery, are actually perceived as a catastrophic blow that sent many African economies staggering and falling on their own knees. Observing in view of the International Monetary Fund's (IMF) and Enhanced Structural Adjustment facility (ESAF) such as Essential Structural Adjustment Programme (ESAP) in sub-Saharan Africa, Naiman and Watkins (1999: np) observe that:

Developing countries worldwide implementing ESAF programmes have experienced lower economic growth than those who have been outside of the programmes. African countries subject to ESAF programmes have fared even worse with their per capita incomes declining than other countries pursuing ESAF programmes. It will be years before these populations recover the per capita incomes that they had prior to structural adjustment.

Naiman and Atkins (Ibid) further observe that, in sub-Saharan Africa, external debt rose from 58 % in 1988 to 70 % in 1996 as a result of the IMF's ESAF programmes. This has resulted in these developing countries diverting resources from expenditures on health care and education in order to service external debt. Besides, annual real per capita GDP growth averaged 0.0 % (from 4 % annual economic growth in the case of Zimbabwe) and 3 % decline in real per capita incomes for all ESAF countries over the period 1991 – 1995, whereas non-ESAF developing countries experienced, on average 1. 0 % annual real per capita GDP growth (IMF Internal Review 1997: 5). This was indeed a drastic fall for African economies considering that during the first decade of independence, the African economies showed modest growth as investment and savings ranged from 15 % to 20 % of the GDP (Chisinga 2010; Mawere and Mubaya 2016). Again, in sub-Saharan Africa, countries that adopted ESAP were "forced," as a matter of policy, to reduce government spending, eliminate government subsidies, privatise government enterprises, and liberalise their economies. This worsened human condition and made Africa one of the most afflicted regions in the world. The ESAP policies adopted by Africa, thus, were both risky and costly in political and social terms as they saw more poverty and underdevelopment towering Africa than any other time before as many people losing their jobs and prices of commodities rising sharply due to uplifting of government subsidies. Worse still, the effects of such policies as ESAP, continue to be felt even today, some years after its inception and implementation in many African countries (for example, Zimbabwe), where the policy prescriptions that came with structural adjustment packages were largely based on a narrow quantitative concern for economic growth and macro-economic stability with little or no concern for qualitative issues of social policy and development such as equity, livelihoods, and human security (cf. Mawere 2011). It is against this backdrop that one can argue that African Framework of Social Policy has failed Africa, for instead of adopting foreign policies such as ESAP, Africa should have come up with its own context-based policy of development.

Moreover, though since the inception of the 2003 SPF there is growing recognition by scholars, African governments and development agencies in both policy and practice that the greatest wealth of a nation is its people, the human capabilities of the African people have not been harnessed and mobilised for the continent's development (see also AU Conference of Ministers 2008). In fact, in most African countries there is relatively low expenditure and investment in social development. There is also little inter-sectorial coordination and cooperation among the various social sector institutions, and between them and the economic ministries (Ibid: 7). This tends to be the case at both policy formulation and implementation stages. In addition, despite the growing recognition by scholars and development agencies that the greatest wealth of a nation is its people, the human capabilities of the African people have not been harnessed and mobilised for the continent's development. Instead, there has emerged in the continent what can be referred to "social exclusion" and to the emergency of an enclave economy – one that deliberately excludes and exploits the majority of the African population while benefiting a minority (Ibid). Social exclusion is a condition experienced by particular groups of people, individuals, households, communities, countries and regions (common in policy discourse) as a result of unequal power relationships in the following main dimensions – economic, political, social and cultural (Popay *et al* 2008). As could be seen, social development policies in the continent are often inadequate because they are oriented towards the urban centres and lack bottom-up concern, with emphasis on decentralisation, self-reliance and community or grass-root involvement. The key messages to African governments is that its governments should address inequalities in areas of health, politics, economics and culture by making sure that social policies are carefully designed, effectively implemented and monitored at all levels.

Also, although the 2003 African Union Policy Framework and Plan of Action on Ageing (AU-Plan) urge the development of strategies to enhance health service provision for Africa's members of the public and older persons (see also UN-HelpAge 2003) as a way to realise their right to health and to encourage their valuable contributions to families and societies, nothing much has been done by many African governments to improve human condition, especially the lives of the aged. Only a few countries such as South Africa have active support systems for its senior citizens. As revealed by South Africa Yearbook (2014/2015), South African government's social security and assistance system is one of the largest in Africa with its spending on social grants system accounting for 3 % of the Gross Domestic Product (GDP). In countries like Mozambique, such support systems as existent in South Africa do not exist (Personal Communication 2013). The same applies to Zimbabwe, where although Departments like Social Welfare exists, the senior citizens are not afforded anything in terms of basic provisions such as food, shelter and clothing mainly due to the overburdening of government by poverty (see also Mawere 2011). Even the so-called pensioners struggle to get their pensions besides that the monthly allowances they get are too meagre. Worse still, the general public remain at risk health-wise. In a recent report on sub-Saharan Africa, for example, it has been revealed that sub-Saharan Africa also bears the brunt of global health inequalities, with high levels of under-nutrition, 50% of maternal and child deaths, and a high burden of infectious diseases, including HIV and AIDS, malaria, and tuberculosis (WHO 2006; Rispel *et al* 2009). All these manifestations are a clear testimony that SPF of Africa has, and indeed, is failing in areas of social security.

Besides, despite the progress made so far on the African continent in terms of socio-economic development, the general social and developmental crises in the continent has remained the same and worsened in some instances. This is in spite of the fact that Africa is endowed with large reserves of natural resources and tracts of arable land suitable for agriculture. As of 19 March 2016, 33 countries of the 48 least developed countries (LDCs) were in Africa, while 9 are found in Asia, 5 in Pacific Island nations and only one in Latin America (Shwayder 2013). By LDC, we mean a country that according to the United Nations, exhibits the lowest indicators of socio-economic development, with the lowest Human Development Index (HDI) ratings of all countries in the continent (UN-OHRLLS 2001). Indeed, it is now universal knowledge that a third of Sub-Saharan Africans are underfed and that more than 40 percent live in absolute poverty as measured by the poverty threshold of less than US$1, 035 per day (UN-OHRLLS 2015). This tragic condition in Africa is caused by many factors, including a high disease burden, poor governance, corruption, rural-urban migration, population explosion, lack of basic infrastructure, and unequal distribution of land and resources found therein, among other reasons. Among many African countries, South Africa, continue experiencing unequal distribution of land. As Cherryl Walker of PLAAS (2013) observes:

> In 1994, as a result of colonial dispossession and apartheid, 87 % of the land was owned by whites and only 13 % by blacks. By 2012 post-apartheid land reform had transferred 7.95 million hectares into black ownership (Nkwinti 2012), which is equivalent, at best, to 7.5 % of formerly white-owned land. Whites as a social category still own most of the country's land and redressing racial imbalances in land ownership is land reform's most urgent priority.

In other African countries like Botswana, Zambia, and Namibia, among others, landlord-tenant relationship continue prevailing in commercial farms, while in Zimbabwe, where "fast track" land reforms have been effected, there is still disproportionate distribution of land among the citizens (Smith 2013). All these manifestations are a clear testimony that SPF in Africa is failing.

In addition to the above, because the top-bottom approach is still prevailing across many African countries, there is still lack of balance of participation between government and its partners in development – like NGOs and donors. This imbalance is chiefly because of Africa's colonial history. In fact, the coming in of the partners on the stage, which are mainly from those countries that were once involved in the colonial project in Africa, have instilled a sense of scepticism in many African governments making them remaining at the centre stage (and partners in the periphery) of development project, thereby promoting a lack of *inclusive* development and participation balance between government and its partners. As the AU Conference of Ministers (2008) aptly puts it:

This lack of 'inclusive' development has pertained to most of Africa's history, and necessitates that the continent develop a social policy framework combining economic dynamism (including pro-poor growth policies), social integration (societies that are inclusive, stable, just and based on the promotion and protection of all human rights, non-discrimination, respect for diversity and participation of all people) and an active role for government in the provision of basic social and other services at local and national levels (p.7).

Thus, the lack of political will on the part of African national governments frustrate attempts at cooperation with 'serious' partners.

Nevertheless, it should be underscored that besides failures, challenges and pitfalls of SPF in Africa elaborated above, Africa has, in the last decade, made significant strides in certain areas of social and economic development. For example, in addition to increasing literacy rates, increasing economic integration through regional groups such as the Economic Community of West African States (ECOWAS), the Southern African Development Corporation (SADC) and the East African Community (EAC), the continent has witnessed increasing democratisation, reduction of gender inequality and civil strife. As Makgoba (1999) points out in view of regional economic integration, economic integration which aligns with the 2003 SPF for Africa, has both political and socio-economic benefits which include strengthening of democratic structures, social security, peace and stability, and economic development. Economically, regional integration has witnessed recovery in the rates of economic growth in Africa with her economies continuing to sustain the growth momentum, recording an overall real GDP growth rate of around 5 % or above (see AU Conference of Ministers 2008). The May 2013 Agenda 2063 by AU is indeed a step of SPF for Africa towards "the Africa we want" with inclusive economic growth, sustainable development, free trade, common market, free movement of people, peace, and foreign-aid independency (see also Mawere and Mubaya 2016).

Furthermore, while the HIV prevalence rate remains high relative to other regions of the world, African countries are making significant progress in reducing or slowing the spread of the epidemic, and access to treatment for people living with the virus and the disease, is improving. African countries like South Africa, Zimbabwe and Mozambique, among others, have either Basic Education Assistance Module (BEAM) (for example, Zimbabwe) or free primary education (for example, Mozambique) and free health care facility and child support grant for its poor citizens in the countryside (for example, South Africa). Overall, countries are intensifying their interventions to improve social development indicators across the continent, with a number having demonstrated their commitment in this direction by creating ministries specially dedicated to social development (AU Conference for Ministers 2008).

Conclusion

To conclude this chapter, it should be emphasised that the African framework of social policy has, since its inception in 2003, made great strides towards improving human condition in many areas such as health, education, gender discourse, economics and politics, among others. However, a lot more is still desired to be done if Africa is to fully realise social security, socio-economic sustainable development and political peace or improved human condition in general. How to achieve this is the object of the next chapter of this book.

Chapter 9

Climate Change and Environmental Management Strategies in Africa

"Climate change is both natural and anthropogenic, but the geographical location and poverty situation of Africa will always make her more vulnerable than any other continent on earth" (Mawere 2016).

Introduction

Since the Second World War, climate change has caused a quandary of problems thereby becoming a menace to the nations of the world. It has, for instance, caused serious environmental change and affected the socio-economic development of many societies especially those in the developing world. While even the industrialised countries of the global south have been affected by climate, the impact of climate change has been worse in Africa than anywhere else in the world due to various factors which include geographical location, poverty, poor technology, and lack of adaptive capacity, among others. Also, environmental change on the continent has exacerbated the development gridlock of the African continent such that its drivers and impacts are worth studying.

That said, this chapter assesses the impact of climate change on socio-economic development in Africa, but realising their plenteousness which in fact would need a whole book to capture comprehensively, only a selected number of impacts will be assessed. In this whole attempt, the chapter begins by shading more light on the conceptualisation of the concepts of 'climate change' and 'environmental change' before looking at the drivers of the latter. Last but not least, the chapter looks at climate change adaptation and mitigation in Africa in view of the threats posed and opportunities opened up by climate change.

Climate Change

Climate change (also known as global warming) has caused a lot of changes on the environment and in human life over the years. These changes – generally referred to as environmental changes – have become a cause of concern prompting the need for environmental management strategies especially in Africa where the changes seem to be more visible and pronounced than elsewhere in the world. Climate change in Africa, thus, has become a thorn in the flesh. But what exactly do we mean by climate change?

Climate change has been notoriously understood such that a plethora of interpretations have been conjured throughout history. The term "climate change" was proposed in 1966 by the World Metrological Organisation (WMO) to refer to all forms of climatic variability on time-scales longer than 10 years, whether the cause was natural or anthropogenic (Hulme 2016). However, since the 1966 the term "climate change" has enjoyed a plethora of interpretations. The Intergovernmental Panel on Climate Change (IPCC) (2007) has, for instance, defined climate change as a change in the state of the climate that can be identified by changes in the mean and/or the variability of its properties, and that persists for an extended period, typically decades or longer. By climate we mean the long-term average weather conditions usually taken over a period of more than 30 years of a region including typical weather patterns such as the frequency and intensity of storms, cold spells, and heat waves (AMCEN, 2011). For the United Nations Framework Convention on Climate Change (UNFCCC), climate change refers to a change of climate that is attributed directly or indirectly to human activity that alters the composition of the global atmosphere and that is in addition to natural climate variability observed over comparable time periods (Ibid). It is worth noting that though the definitions of climate change vary in diction and semantics, they seem to all agree that climate change encompasses changes in climatic conditions over time, whether natural or human induced. Also, it is widely agreed that while climate change may occur naturally, it is generally agreed that anthropogenic factors are the main causes. These changes have impacted on both the environment – environmental change – and human life both negatively and positively as shall be explained in this chapter. Yet before looking on the impacts of climate change on the environment, we should first of all understand what we mean by environmental change.

Environmental change

Environmental change has been semantically defined differently by scholars and organisations though the meaning has technically remained the same. The Centre for Disease Control and Prevention (CDC) (2016), for example, has defined environmental change as a physical or material change to the economic, social, or physical environment. This understanding of environmental change resonates with that of Johnson *et al* (1997), who define it as a disturbance of the environment most often caused by human influences and natural ecological processes. By environment, we mean the sum total of all surroundings of a living organism, including natural forces and other living things, which provide conditions for development and growth as well as of danger and damage (Business Dictionary, n.d) to the organism in question. What the definitions of environmental change above by CDC and Johnson *et al* entail is that environmental change is both natural and human (or animal) induced to include phenomena such as climate change, natural disasters, human (or animal interference), and infestation of invasive species, among others (Ibid). But as noted earlier in the introduction, part of the objective of this chapter is to critically examine the anthropogenic drivers (causes/initiators) of environmental change and how they can be addressed for purposes of both sustainability and perpetuation of life on earth.

Drivers of environmental change: Impacts and solutions

Over the years, environmental change has become a cause of concern at national, continental and global levels. While environmental change – just like climate change – is believed to have always been taking place even in a natural environment without human beings, anthropogenic activities have been singled out as the main drivers of environmental change. These have come to be known as anthropogenic drivers of environmental change. Anthropogenic drivers of environmental change are many. For purposes of this book, focus shall be made on the major anthropogenic drivers of environmental change in Africa which broadly include technological, economic, demographic, conflict and civil unrest, social, and political ([bad] governance). In this whole attempt, we begin by shading more light on environmental change before critically examining the aforementioned anthropogenic (or human induced) drivers of environment change in Africa and how each of them can be addressed.

To start with the anthropogenic driver, technology, one notes that this has become more of a paradox in the sense that it has brought both positive and negative change to both human life and the environment in general. In fact technology has become a force that can tear the environment apart and a force that binds the environment together. We are however worried about the negative change that technology has caused (and continue to cause) on the environment. Technology, whose meaning is unstable, has been widely and commonly understood as "all tools, machines, utensils, weapons, instruments, housing, clothing, communicating and transporting devices, and the skills by which we produce and use them" (Bain 1937: 860). While technology has helped develop more advanced economies and allowed the rise of a leisure class, many technological processes produce unwanted by-products, known as pollution besides that they deplete natural resources (Liddell & Scott 1980). Some like obsolete technology (such as used vehicles pollute the environment while others like nuclear weapon cause serious damage to both life and the natural environment as what happened in 1945 at Hiroshima and Nagasaki (in Japan) when nuclear bombs were used. More other technologies such as the biotechnology of genetic engineering have already caused moral and health outcries in African countries such as South Africa and Zimbabwe, through the production of genetically modified foods (GMOs) and cloning (in human beings). Realising the dangers of GMOs technology, Zimbabwe has even banned their importation into the country from South Africa (see Kwinika 2010; Chawafambira 2013; Made 2016). All these are a tip of an ice bag in as far as the negative impacts of technology are concerned. The problem that remains boggling human minds today is how to address the problems caused by technology given its paradoxical nature explained above and the fact that it appears to be a no-turning back development?

In response to this concern, scholars like Francis Fukuyama (2002; 1992) have warned humanity to desist from engaging in technologies that introduce unprecedented new challenges to both human beings and the environment. He argues in his *Our posthuman future ...* (2002) that as a result of biomedical advances, we are facing the possibility of a future in which our humanity itself (*and indeed our environment*) will be altered beyond recognition. On the same note, I argue that one way of addressing the challenges brought by technology is to ban all technologies that are detrimental to life and the environment as has been done with GMOs technology in Zimbabwe.

The other way out of the problem is to encourage scientists to blend technology with morality so that they abstain from all technologies that harm (or have the potential to harm) the environment and any form of life on earth. The point here is that scientists should only be encouraged to engage in technology that is not harmful to the environment and life on earth. Thus, in view of development studies, all technology should support human development but in an ethical and environmentally friendly manner that promotes life and sustainable development.

Another major anthropogenic driver of environmental change related to technology is demography particularly, the rapid population growth (or what others call population explosion). With the advancement of science and technology, child mortality and maternity death rates have been greatly reduced across the globe. While positive, this has triggered a rapid increase in population growth with Africa in the lead. In fact, while some parts of the world are witnessing smaller increments of population growth, and some like Germany, Japan and Spain, are experiencing population decreases, Africa's population is projected by the United Nations Population Division to accelerate such that by 2050, annual increases will exceed 42 million people per year, and total population will have doubled to 2. 4 billion (Bish 2016) if nothing is done to arrest population increase on the continent. It is worth noting that population growth has adverse effects on the natural environment through increased pollution of the environment, overexploitation of natural resources, and poor farming practices. As Debasish (n.d) observes, rapid population growth leads to environmental change, particularly through destruction of forests, wetlands, and other ecologically sensitive areas. In fact, rapid population growth in Africa has swelled the ranks of unemployed men and women at an alarming rate. Due to this, a large number of people are being pushed in ecologically sensitive areas such as hill sides and tropical forests leading to the cutting of forests for cultivation, which in turn results in severe environmental change. Cases in point in Africa include some parts of southeastern Zimbabwe and southern Mozambique where people are encroaching mountain hills and stream banks for farming (cf. Mawere 2013; 2015). Besides all this, the increasing population growth leads to the migration of large numbers of people to urban areas for jobs resulting in polluted air, water, and noise in towns and cities.

The problem of demography as it negatively impacts the environment can be addressed by population control through healthcare education and the use of birth control methods. As noted by Debasish (n.d), as of 2014, most countries in the third world are faced with the problem of uncontrolled population growth. If not checked, the challenge could lead to resource depletion while measures such as recycling of used non-biodegradable materials if not adopted may result in land pollution. Thus, as further noted by Debasish, the problem of land pollution that normally results from overpopulation could be dealt with by recycling used non-biodegradable materials such as plastics and metal scraps.

The third prime anthropogenic driver of environmental change in Africa is the economic activity as manifested through activities such as agriculture, mining, and industry. These activities, though, are also understood as crucial contributors to economic growth, have detrimental effects to the natural environment if wrongly and/or excessively practised as is the cases in many African countries such as Zimbabwe, Mozambique, Zambia, the Democratic Republic of Congo, among others. For example, unsustainable agriculture practices such as monocropping, commercial fertiliser use, pesticide use, genetic engineering, intensive irrigation (which leads to salinisation), slash and burn, cultivation of sensitive areas such as wetlands, industrial agriculture, stream bank cultivation and steep slope cultivation, present immediate threat to species and ecosystems around the world. Industrial agriculture, for instance, pollutes air, water and soil while at the same time reduces biodiversity and contributes to climate change (cf. van der Warf and Petit 2002; Grace Communications Foundation 2014). Mining, on the other hand, can result in water and land pollution as well as environmental change through deserted mine pits, use of chemicals for mineral processing, and contamination of natural water (through mercury) which may cause widespread killing of aquatic life as happened in 2000 and 2010/2011 in Mozambique when gold panners in the Munhena Mining site (in Manica Province) contaminated Lucite River (Mawere 2011; see also Brereton & Forbes 2004).

Although difficult to address given the paradoxical nature of economic activity, both as a stimulant of development and as a threat to the natural environment, the problems that this anthropogenic activity poses to the environment can still be addressed. The problems posed by economic activity, be it mining, agriculture or industry, can be addressed through promotion of sustainable management in all these areas – for example, sustainable agriculture, sustainable mining and sustainable industrial development. Promoting sustainability does not only lessen the negative effects posed by the activities but also promote sustainable development. By sustainable development, we mean development that meets the needs of the present without compromising the ability of future generations to meet their needs (Brundtland Commission 1987). Taking an example of industrial crop production, this can be avoided by making use of sustainable alternatives to industrial crop production such as conservation agriculture, zero/no-till agricultural methods, organic fertilisers, and innovative pest management approaches. In some parts of Zimbabwe such as Hwange and Hurungwe, some farmers have already adopted the zero tillage agricultural method as a measure to reduce environmental change (cf. Moyo 2010; Bafana 2013).

Besides the three drivers discussed above, social dimension has also been recognised as one of the major drivers of environmental change in Africa. In many rural areas of the developing countries such as those of Africa, social inequality including in areas of gender, has caused or perpetuated poverty. Poverty, on the other hand, has resulted in the overdependence on natural resources and consequently their overexploitation of resources. As Planas (2012) noted, today, about 80 % of the world's energy consumption is sustained by the extraction of fossil fuels, which consists of oil, coal, firewood, and gas. These fossil fuels pollute the environment – water, air and land. Gasses emitted to the atmosphere, for example, contribute to the destruction of the ozone layer.

Such a problem could be addressed by simply shifting from pollution fuels and sources of energy – firewood, coal and paraffin – to alternative pollution-free sources of energy such as solar especially in the tropical countries such as Zimbabwe (or Africa in general) where sunshine is in abundance. Afforestation and re-afforestation could also help to contain environmental change given that trees help to absorb and utilise some of the gases – carbon dioxide – produced during emissions into the atmosphere. Besides, policies such as "pollute and pay" could also be introduced as a measure to curb and deter potential polluters of the environment.

Also, the fifth major driver of environmental change is poor governance or politics in general. Poor governance in issues of the environment is normally manifested through non-existence of or weak environmental policies, laws, and institutions as well as corruption. Corruption, for example, which is the abuse of public power for private gain (World Bank 1997) is detrimental to environmental stability in that it results in bad policy formulation, management and enforcement as well as organised crimes, some of which ruinously affect the environment (cf. Robbins 2000; Carter 1997; Damania *et al* 2003).

As has been highlighted above, non-existent or weak environmental policies, laws and institutions as well as corruption normally result in ineffective implementation of environmental laws and policies. This cascades into poor environmental management as is currently exemplified by the Environment Management Agency (EMA) in Zimbabwe. While EMA is mandated to manage the environment on behalf of the government, it has since been recognised as a weak institution that ineffectively implements environmental laws and policies, hence the rapid environmental change in many parts of Zimbabwe. Thus, to address the problem of environmental change at national level, Zimbabwe (through its agencies such as EMA) will need to reorient its employees dealing with environmental issues. This measure is applicable to other African countries too. Elsewhere, I observed that Mozambique is facing serious challenges of environmental change due to weak environmental management system (Mawere 2011; 2013). Environmental management could be enhanced through workshops, staff development programmes, retraining of environmental officers, and environmental awareness campaigns.

Last but not least among the major drivers of environmental change in Africa is conflict and civil unrest. As noted by the World Bank (2008), in war zones, there is no or lack of control such that gas emissions, deforestation, land and water pollution are high. With regard to Africa, the World Bank gives examples of Burundi, Somalia and Rwanda, countries which due to conflict and civil unrest, have recorded high negative environmental changes due to no or lack of rule of law. As the DFID (1997: 16) report notes "violent conflict generates social division, reverses economic progress, impedes sustainable development, and frequently results in human rights violations. Large population movements triggered by conflict threaten the security and livelihood of the whole region." Part of what the DFID reports was witnessed during the 1994 Rwandan genocide which drove people in masses into the forest, thereby causing more environmental damage and/or change resulting from overexploitation of forest resources and bomb explosions. It is estimated that nearly 2 million Hutus fled Rwanda with approximately 720, 000 of these refugees settling in refugee camps on the fringes of Virunga National Park, the first United Nations World Heritage site declared endangered due to an armed conflict, as the refugees stripped off an estimated 35 square kilometres of forest for firewood and shelter-building materials (cf. Worldwatch Institute 2013; Jones 2001). Such observations are reverberated by DeWeerdt (2008) who argues that modern warfare tactics, as seen in the American war in Vietnam, the Rwandan and Congolese civil wars, and war in Iraq, have greatly increased human capacity to destroy – through firepower – the natural landscape and produce devastating environmental effects on the planet. This also resonates with the Worldwatch's (2013) observation that the deliberate destruction of the environment as a military strategy known as "ecocide" is exemplified by the United States of America (USA) response to guerrilla warfare in Vietnam where in an effort to deprive the communist Viet Cong guerrillas of the dense cover they found in the hardwood forests and mangroves that fringed the Mekong Delta, the USA military sprayed 79 million litres of herbicides and defoliants (including Agent Orange) over about one-seventh of the land area of southern Vietnam. This destroyed about 14 % of hardwood forests in the region thereby threatening biodiversity and altering the vegetation severely.

To address this anthropogenic problem at least at continental level, there is need for Africa to adopt sound conflict management and transformation measures to curb civil unrest and in turn minimise or prevent environmental change on the continent. As Schipper (2007) suggests, such measures could include the engagement of regional blocks and organisations such as African Union (AU), South African Development Cooperation (SADC) and Economic Cooperation of West African Countries (ECOWAS) to negotiate peace and ensure transformation in war zones.

I underscore that while environmental change is believed to have always been taking place even in a natural environment without human beings, anthropogenic activities such as technological, demographic, social, governance and economic activities have been singled out as the main drivers of environmental change in Africa and elsewhere in the world. As has been discussed in this section, these anthropogenic activities should be mitigated against to control climate change in such a way that perpetuation of life on earth is ensured promote sustainable development at a global level is promoted.

Climate change, mitigation and adaptation in Africa

In this section, we start by looking at conceptual issues surrounding climate change, particularly climate change adaptation in terms of how this differs from climate change mitigation. Thereafter, we look at the challenges brought about by climate change before we finally look at opportunities opened up by climate change.

Climate change adaptation

This is one of the two policy responses – mitigation and adaptation – to climate change which seeks to lower the risks posed by the consequences of climate change (Fisher 2012). This means that while mitigation addresses the root causes of climate change by reducing greenhouse gas emissions, adaptation tries to come up with ways and mechanisms to reduce the risks caused by the consequences of climate change. A good example of climate change adaptation is when people grow drought resistant crops in an attempt to adapt to climate change. So is when they adopt irrigation schemes in drought prone areas.

What is important to remember here is that when mitigating, we are attacking the actual causes of climate change, for example, gas emissions whereas when adapting we are trying to come up with mechanisms/ways to cope with the effects/problems or negative impacts caused by climate change. I should also underline that adaptation measures can be planned in advance to reduce the vulnerability to the people (Fisher 2012).

The impact of climate change on the socio-economic development in Africa

I have already noted with concern that since the Second World War, climate change has become a menace to the nations of the world. It has affected the socio-economic development of many societies especially those in the developing world. The impact of climate change has however been worse in Africa than anywhere else in the world due to various factors such as geographical location, poverty, poor technology and lack of adaptive capacity. It is in this view that it becomes peremptory to assess the impact of climate change on socio-economic development in Africa.

To start with the negative impacts – which in fact are social, economic, healthy, political, and environmental –, climate change is already causing temperature changes in many parts of Africa and the world beyond. This in turn is causing health, socio-economic, and environmental problems. As Hellmuth *et al* (2007: v) notes "climate change is resulting in rising sea-levels, droughts, and famine, and the loss of up to a third of the world's plant and animal species." These problems posed by climate change such as drought, floods and others impact negatively on the socio-economic development in Africa as they divert the attention of the African people in engaging in projects that aim at improving their social status and economic well-being as they spent more energy in looking for solutions to handle the climate related problems.

More so, climate change has already been pronounced as "a security threat to Africa" (FAO 2008: 7). In fact, Africa especially the sub-Saharan Region is already experiencing a series of droughts and famines as well as storms, floods, and cyclones which are all a big threat and cause of concern to the security of the people of Africa. In the recent years, for example, Zimbabwe and the larger part of southern Africa have experienced serious droughts notably in the years 1992, 2003/2004, 2007/2008, and 2015/2016. Mozambique, as with many parts of southern Africa, has also suffered a series of floods and cyclones – cyclone Eline and Japhet – over the recent past, notably in 2000, 2002, and 2011 (Mawere 2011; RSMC La Reunion Report 2014; Christie & Halon 2001). These cyclones have resulted in land degradation. Besides causing land degradation (UN 2005), diseases such as malaria and diarrhoea (ReliefWeb 2000), the cyclones have destroyed properties and infrastructure such as roads, schools, hospitals, houses and livestock. As recorded by RSMC (2014), about US$ 500 Million worth of property was damaged, approximately 700 people were killed, about 463, 000 people were displaced or left homeless, and 20, 000 herds of cattle were lost during the 2000 floods in Mozambique. Thus, looking at the damage and suffering inflicted during the Mozambican floods, there is no doubt that climate change has a negative impact to socio-economic development.

Besides, climate change has been said to cause various skin ailments such as skin cancer, "skin rush," and mild blindness especially to the very young and the elderly (IPCC 2007). This is believed to be a result of the increased amount of sun rays due to the destruction of the ozone layer by fossil gas emissions. The Third Assessment Report of the Intergovernmental Panel on Climate Change (2001) reveals that the global average temperature will increase by 1. 4 to 5. 8 Degrees Celsius between 1900 and 21 000 if the levels of emissions are not reduced, causing a range of diseases, food insecurity, and loss of life. This will in no doubt impact negatively on Africa's socio-economic development given that for any country to socio-economically develop it has to have a health working class. Ailing youths will already been a liability and not an asset to instil and propel socio-economic development on the continent.

Furthermore, climate change is believed to be already exacerbating the levels of poverty through drought, famine, and floods in Africa (Ibid; Fisher 2012) where adaptive capacity is low due to the already existing high levels of poverty and poor technology. As Fisher (2012) tells us, as the societies of the world experience climatic shifts in temperature, flooding, and storm frequency, low income countries such as those of Africa tend to be more vulnerable to climate risks. These risks and problems are already increasing the vulnerability of youths especially the young women and girls to prostitution and HIV/AIDS as economic levels in African countries such as Zimbabwe deepen and food insecurity escalates, thereby impacting negatively on the socio-economic development of the continent.

In addition to the above, climate change has become a big challenge to sustainable development. Sustainable development is development that meets the needs of the present without compromising the ability of future generations to meet their own needs (Brundtland Commission Report 1987). As Kyte (2014) notes, climate change is a challenge to sustainable development because it already threatens to drag millions of people into grinding poverty yet we have never had better know-how and solutions to avert the crisis caused by climate change. It also threatens to affect human industry such as tourism which has a negative bearing on socio-economic development. McMichael and Woodruff (2006) captures this aptly when they observe that climate change affect most of the African tourism industries – such as Gonarezhou, Kruger, and Gorongoza National Parks in Zimbabwe, South Africa and Mozambique respectively – which largely depend on climatic conditions to sustain their scenery, flora and fauna.

However, while the impact of climate change on the socio-economic development in Africa are overwhelming as elaborated above, it should be borne in mind that there are also opportunities created by climate change which seem to impact positively on the continent's socio-economic development. The first opportunity created by climate change is business for some companies such as those which deal with global disasters related to weather. This is aptly captured by Jennison (2014) who notes, climate change offers business opportunities for some companies such electrical energy production companies and companies dealing with global disasters related to weather. In Africa as elsewhere in the world, such companies normally create new jobs in the energy sector, which in turn enhance socio-economic development of the people of Africa, hence the positives of climate change.

Secondly, climate change offers opportunities to the private sector to work with national governments in areas of innovation, food aid, agriculture (especially irrigation farming or mechanised farming in general), and other such development projects. In Zimbabwe, for example, droughts and famine in the recent past have created an opportunity for many Non-governmental organisations such as CARE International, USAID, World Vision, Heifer International, among others, to work with the government in development projects such as livestock breeding, poultry, horticulture and many others which do not only seek to boost the socio-economic development of the Zimbabwean people, but also to transfer technology from the global north to the global south. Now, given that such opportunities are opened up as a result of climate change, one would argue that in a way, climate change help to create opportunities for the enhancement of the socio-economic lives of the African people.

Thirdly, climate change creates opportunities for scientists to engage in further research. As noted by Mawere (2014; 2015), weather related problems posed by climate change have prompted some communities in Africa to devise their own indigenous coping mechanisms to counter or lessen the severity of climate change in their localities. Due to increasing temperature changes and outages of electricity in Nigeria (as we are currently experiencing here in Zimbabwe), communities in Jigawa State of northern Nigeria developed an efficient electricity-free 'refrigerator' – what has come to be better known as the "Jigawa Pot-in-Pot Cooling System." The system consists of two different-sized earthenware pots, one inside the other. The space between the pots is filled with water-retentive sand. Perishable food such as tomatoes, green pepper, eggplants and other products, is placed in the smaller pot (inside) and covered with a cloth. The pots are placed in a dry, ventilated place and the sand is periodically watered. As the water in the sand evaporates, into the drier air outside, it cools the pots and their contents. Using this method, it is said that tomatoes and green pepper can be kept fresh for up to 3 weeks while eggplants can be kept fresh for up to a month (see Mawere 2014). The method is helping farmers to avoid loses during time when their crops reach peak periods and face risks of rotting. It is also said that ¾ of the population in Jigawa State are using this system. Thus, climate change can open opportunities for scientists in Africa to engage in further research, which in turn improve the socio-economic well-being of the people of Africa as exhibited in the example here in explained.

Conclusion

The negative impacts of climate change are more than evident in Africa, particularly with respect to the natural environment and the socio-economic development in the continent. As has been discussed in this chapter, there are a number of problems posed by climate change, which range from social to health, political, environmental and economic. However, one should bear in mind the fact that besides the negativities associated with climate change, the latter also creates opportunities for socio-economic development in Africa as had been explained in this chapter.

Chapter 10

Building Blocks of Development: Towards a Framework of Development for Africa

"It pays to copy but only when one copies good things" (Munyaradzi Mawere 2016).

Introduction

The main problem at the centre of Africa's underdevelopment has been the problem of copying. Right from the birth of national independence in the 1960s, Africa has been copying its former colonial masters. It has been copying almost everything from the administrative strategies to the constitution, development policies, epistemic theories, and development models and theories. While copying sometimes pays, it only pays when one copies good things. The unfortunate thing with Africa is that it has copied even the bad things and in many cases the worst things simply because they come from the West – their former colonial masters. It has copied the corruption syndrome that the former European colonisers used to exploit Africa's resources. It has copied the autocratic, despotic and repressive governance that the colonial administrators used to subjugate the people of Africa. It has copied the education curricular of the former European colonisers even if the curricular were meant to ensure bottle neck education, and were only theoretical to arrest the spirit of development on the continent. It has copied the culture of the former European colonisers even when the culture is so individualistic and capitalistic to the extent of the head of families wanting to sell to the family members what they produce together. The list is endless. But why continue copying when the majority of the things being copied are negative? Wouldn't this be described as foolhardiness at its best? Isn't it as foolish as walking into a snake-pit barefooted and with eyes wide open? The wise often say he who crosses a crocodile infested river risks getting attacked. So is he who jumps a raging fire. One wonders if something becomes correct when it is indeed worst in the eyes of logic and reason simply because it comes from the West! Why I am troubling the question of copying here when discussing the question of development and underdevelopment in Africa?, one might ask.

To start with, Africa is a continent richly and judiciously endowed with both natural resources and human capital of quality. Ridiculously, it is the poorest and most underdeveloped continent in the world. Two immediate grand questions that come to mind are: 'Why Africa remains on the brinks of development to the extent of legging behind other continents? And, how to build Africa from inside in a way that fosters the continent's own development and sustainability?' These questions, though have gained tremendous prominence in both the corporate world and intellectual discourse over the years, no lasting remedial solutions have so far been proffered to effectively and meticulously deal with Africa's sustainability predicament once and for all. This is in spite of the fact that the problem has been persistent and a wide array of solutions suggested since Africa's independence from European colonialism through the present. Given the nebulous nature coupled with the contested possible causes of Africa's towering ghost of underdevelopment, a robust comprehension of "underdevelopment" and analysis of its root causes as a troubling phenomenon on the continent calls into question the role and position of Corporate Africa and other such stakeholders in the whole matrix of Africa's sustainability agenda. Drawing on literature and my research findings in the recent past, this chapter critically seeks to account for the various insinuations on why Africa legs behind other continents development-wise. It further suggests possible ways on how a vicarious *volte-face* could be achieved to allow Africa to get on its own wheels and catch-up with other continents while fostering sustainability and sanity. This re-examination of how to build Africa from within is executed on the pretext that the enjoyment of sustainable socio-economic development, justice, and peace in Africa, as elsewhere in the world, is closely linked to a socially, politically and economically participative *local* corporate world alongside other stakeholders.

The African development predicament: Towards building a "new Africa"

The question on the African development predicament cannot be answered in a word. This is because, complex and protracted as it is, there is no one solution to the problem. In this book, I provide what I consider as the major steps that Africa could and should take if she is ever to achieve development in the continent as a whole. My suggested solutions to the African development predicament are thus as follow:

i). Unity of purpose as a continent

Africa's natural resources have been largely monopolised by American and European companies since the trans-Atlantic period and the colonial era through the present times. More recently, China has joined in. This exploitation of resources has been made possible by the African situation mainly disunity and poverty. Europe and America have capitalised on the poverty that characterise many [un-united] African countries to enter into business deal where there former always come out as winners and never as losers or equal partners. To avoid such asymmetrical and exploitative relationships, Africa should unite and do away with colonial boarders while coming up with a common framework of development. The United States of America have successfully done this, which partly explains why she is considered one of the economic and political giants of the world.

This is not a new proposal to the African development predicament. Many African states and development theorists alike, have for a long time proposed the need for a United States of Africa. As early as 1957, Kwame Nkrumah, for example, suggested that African countries rally together as a country – one nation, one continent. Nkrumah revealed the need for this unity of purpose right at the eve of Ghana's independence in 1957 when he declared that:

> The unity of purpose will enable African countries, both those in the coastal regions and the landlocked ones, to redistribute their wealth and resources evenly to ensure development of the whole continent.

Besides, unity of purpose will allow African governments to channel the money being used in the processing of visas, paying duty for goods imported from neighbouring countries, and in safe-guarding [colonial] boarders towards developmental projects. In other words, unity of purpose will save Africa large quantities of money that is currently spend on border posts and security across the continent.

ii). Africa to produce visionary borderless leaders

Related to point number (i) above is the need for Africa to produce visionary borderless leaders who think beyond their national boundaries. As has been argued in many parts of this book, a divided Africa will reach nowhere both politically and economically before falling on its knees. I push this argument further noting that Africa as a continent needs leaders who have a continent wide development mindset, who can facilitate the cooperation in all areas of human development on the continent. This is necessary because an integrated African economy and political entity of global scale is not only formidable but a necessity for the continent's success, progress and wholesome development. There is, therefore, the need for Africa to produce leaders who think beyond their national boundaries: leaders with the zeal to work together for the creation of a more cohesive and integratory continent that benefits all its populations regardless of their status or class.

iii). Establish a strong industrial base in Africa

A country without a strong industrial base can hardly provide employment for its entire people. Unfortunately, this is the situation that obtains in many African countries where the industrial base is not only poor but where industries are found mainly in the urban areas. This has resulted in overcrowding conditions in many African cities due to massive rural to urban migration. This calls for the need not only to widen the industrial base in many African urban areas, but to also to establish rural industries to create jobs for the rural folk while curbing rural – urban migration (i.e. thru corporate Africa and establishment of industries to utilise natural resources). Africa can for example learn from China. Although China's state, at one time or another suffered the authoritarian excesses of Tiananmen of 1989 and the current paranoia regarding social dissent, it has been capable of avoiding serious social and economic cataclysmic situations as those engulfing the larger part of Africa. African leaders, therefore, have much to learn from China. As the Nigerian author, Chinua Achebe, once said of his own country, "the Nigerian problem is the unwillingness or inability of its leaders to rise to the responsibility, to the challenge of the personal example, which are the hallmarks of true leadership" (BBC News, 30 November 2015). Thus, Africa may perhaps draw important lessons from the rise of China since the 1980s when the Chinese government introduced the New Economy Policy, which was very experimental and pragmatic to the extent that it employed those models that worked and discarded those that did not work for China.

iv). Liberalisation of domestic market

Related to the point explained above is the need for African countries to liberalise their domestic markets so as to help bridging the gap between the rich and the poor. Countries like Japan has done this successfully by giving liberty to anyone of its citizens to improve on the Toyota model, resulting in many Toyota models produced in Japan over the years. This extension of copyrights from the government to the people (or citizens) has seen Japan's economy growing faster than ever in the past few years. Besides, the move has helped greatly to bridge the gap between the poor and the rich in Japan.

Owing to the successes that liberalisation of domestic market yielded for Japan, I argue that African countries adopt the same so as to promote growth of their respective economies while bridging the gap between the rich and the poor. Unfortunately, this is contrary to the situation that obtains in many African countries. In Zimbabwe, for example, innovation and creativity by citizens have been discouraged as many people who have innovatively came up with guns, aeroplanes and many other technological developments have failed to get support from both the government and non-state actors.

v). Retain skilled human capital in Africa

Skill flight or brain drain of the skilled in Africa is difficult to measure and note with precision. As noted by World Migration (2008), only between the period of 2000 to 2005, an estimated 440, 000 people per year migrated from Africa, most of them to Europe. This has been mainly been a result of the search for "greener pastures" and the grand narrative that education outside of Africa is better than inside' is persistent (Han *et al.*, 2015). This narrative together with the lure for high paying jobs and scholarship opportunities (Teferra, 1997) continue to entice thousands of Africans to travel outside of the continent for academic development. Only as recent as 2013, the U.S. President Barak Obama in South Africa, in his bid to expand training cooperation, announced the Washington Fellowship for Young African Leaders, "a new programme that is going to give thousands of promising young Africans like you the opportunity to come to the United States and develop your skills at some of our best colleges and universities" (Obama 2013). This kind of gesture has a long history. In fact, since 2007, the US-centric professional engineering organisations, The Institute of the Institute of Electrical and Electronics Engineers (IEEE) – claiming to be the largest professional organisation in the world – and the Semiconductor Industry Association have been lobbying the American government for the "retention of highly educated immigrants as part of a broader competitiveness and innovation initiative" (Scalise & Meredith, 2007: np). In their narrative, the organisations state that "51 percent of master's and 71 percent of Ph.D. graduates in electrical and electronic engineering from U.S. universities are foreign nationals" (Ibid). More so, in a United States of America study surveying foreign-born STEM (Science, Technology, Engineering and Mathematics) graduates, Han *et al.* (2015) show that most graduates (upto 80%) do not return to their home-countries. As McManes (2013) and Patel (2015) noted, given their status as skilled and highly intellectually gifted, they are normally lured with "good" jobs and remunerations, among other things to remain in the United States of America. Yet, considering its effects to the continent of Africa, brain drain should be curbed at all costs to avoid loss of talent.

vi). Decolonise the African curriculum

Many African institutions, universities included, tend to forget that education is generally all about teaching people the right skills to enhance creativity, productivity and exchange of knowledge and skills. This would enable Africa to provide education that suits the African needs. China, for example, has successfully done this, hence coming up with Chinese medicine and a strong industrial base. Why we can't have the African medicine, for example, in the world market?

vii). Tackle poor governance in Africa

Political violence, corruption in its all forms such as nepotism, bribery, embezzlement, and kick-backs should not only be discouraged but stemmed out. Instead, accountability, transparency, and rule of law should be promoted.

Poor governance in many African countries such as Mozambique, Zimbabwe, Burundi, Angola, Uganda, Sudan, Darfur, Somalia and others, has resulted in conflict-torn situations. Such situations have made it very difficult for these countries to develop socio-economically and politically by building infrastructure and promote rule of law and justice.

At another level, the conflict-torn situations in these countries have given neighbouring countries a very big refugee burden, which has dragged their development pace.

viii). Build a strong agricultural base in Africa

In the past, especially around the 1950s and 1960s, emphasis for development was placed on the need for industrialisation at the expense of agricultural development. Since the 1990s, this mindset is fast changing, with agricultural development being seen as an important of any development strategy. This is because agriculture produce cash crops for foreign currency generation, produce raw materials to help industry, employs a large percentage of labour force, and most importantly produce food to meet the nutritional needs of the population (cf. Addison-Wesley 2009). Besides, it is well known that more than half of the world population lives in the rural areas, where there is rapid population growth, high unemployment rates and wide spread poverty. Thus, developing a strong agricultural base with special focus on small holder farmers in the rural area will put the continent on a better position to feeds its people while creating employment for them. This will also go a long way in addressing inequalities between the rural people and their counterparts in the urban areas.

Unfortunately, many African countries have confused land ownership such that land is either underutilised or in the hands of those without the expertise to utilise it to the maximum. This is to say there is unequal distribution of land in many African countries. Furthermore, in those countries where rainfall is unreliable but [fertile] land is in abundance, there has been no or little irrigation taking place. This is underutilisation of the resource, land, which is the most important resource for the promotion of development). A strong agricultural base also promotes a strong industrial base as most of the raw materials used in the industries come from agriculture.

The strong agricultural base in Africa could be developed through a Comprehensive Africa Agriculture Development Programme (CAADP) implementation. While this programme is already in place and obliges all member states to commit 10 % of the national budget to developing agricultural sector, in many African countries such as Zimbabwe, the programme is not supported with sound policy frameworks (cf. Chingwe 2013). In Zimbabwe for example, never has so far the country committed the 10 % of its national budget to agriculture despite the fact that over 70 % of the population derives a livelihood from the agricultural sector while a third of the formal labour force are employed in agriculture-related employment. This programme should also be supported by land tenure security system to encourage farmers to make long term investments in their farms. In fact, security tenure must be provided to all classes of farmers to ensure a meaningful and sustainable participation of private capital in financing agriculture. In Zimbabwe, for instance, the rural land market does not exist at the moment yet it is pivotal in encouraging long-term investments on farms. Besides, land tenure security will help farmers to access lines of credit as they will now have collateral security which they often lack.

ix). Africa to recognise herself as an equal partner

A critical look at Africa's trade relationships with the so-called developed countries reveals that the terms of trade set by richer countries tend to often exploit her. More often than not, unfairly low prices for Africa's exports of commodities to Europe and the United States of America, such as tobacco, coffee, beef, cocoa and other export products are charged.

More so, foreign businesses operating in Africa often do not help the local economy as much as they can and indeed should do to promote development in their host countries. The international policies that should play a pivotal role to end African underdevelopment and poverty by helping African countries to integrate in the global market are not even doing much. The US and European Union, protecting their key industries, especially those that

Africa could compete with like agriculture, they give preferential market conditions to developed countries instead of poor countries like those of Africa.

x). Africa to promote context-based development strategies

Since the 1990s, there has been widespread understanding by development strategists that understanding of people's perspectives and participation by the poor in the development process is a prerequisite for the success of any development project. This people-centred approach to development has been partly driven by the so-called livelihoods approach, a multi-disciplinary approach that focuses above all on the local context as well as the opportunities and constraints that individuals in the context in question face in their attempts to escape from poverty. In fact, it was realised that poverty persists because of the absence of not only national economic growth, but because of lack of involvement and participation of the people. At the same time, it was realised that national economic growth itself can also be inhibited by wide-scale poverty, suggesting that a more direct focus on poverty reduction on the people may lead to a virtuous cycle of poverty reduction and growth. This was a very important observation given that even in countries that are said to be enjoying national economic growth, poverty often remained entrenched and sometimes not reduced quickly enough due to lack of people participation or involvement. This observation was made as a counter to the 1970s approach (and also approach in many countries today) that development strategies should focus more on the government other than on the needs of the poor: an approach which led to liberal market initiatives such as the Economic Structural Adjustment Programmes (ESAPS) in the late 1990s and early 1990s in many of the African countries leading to the demise of their economies. There was need, therefore, to recognise the complexity of development and of the need to craft and tailor policies as well as interventions by both the government and non-governmental development agencies to the particular needs and particular political, social and economic circumstances of the people – human capital – and context in question.

Consequently, many contemporary development initiatives, especially by non-state actors now focus their attention more on the needs of the poor (particularly children and women) rather than just focusing on the productive sectors of the economy of the society in question. This means that there is now more focus on people-based and context-based development initiatives than there is on government-led initiatives. One of Africa's context-based development strategies lies in its indigenous resources.

References

Abercrombie, N., Hill, S. and Turner, B. S. 1994. *The Penguin Dictionary of Sociology* (3rd Ed.), Penguin Group: Penguin Books.

Aborishade, F. 2002. Effects of globalisation on social and labour practices in privatised enterprises in Nigeria, *A Research Report Submitted to the Centre for Advanced Social Sciences*, Port Harcourt: Nigeria.

Albrow, M. & King, E. 1990. (Eds.) *Globalisation, knowledge and society*, Sage Books: London.

Alexander, J. 2006. The *Unsettled Land: State- making & the Politics of Land in Zimbabwe 1893 – 2003*, Weaver Press: Harare.

Adams, W. M. 2006. *The Future of Sustainability: Re-Thinking Environment and Development in the Twenty-First Century*, The World Conservation Union.

AGRA, 2012. 'Investing in agriculture to reduce poverty and hunger', AGRA Alliance.

Ajaz, D. (n.d). The dual economy, Ajaz Debras Topics, Available at: ttps://www.economics.utoronto.ca/ahussain/papers/ajaz_debraj_topics1.pdf. Retrieved on: 22 April 2016.

Akandele, W. 2002. 'Drawback of cultural globalisation,' Available at: www.org/globalisation.com

Alcott, W. (n.d). 'The underdevelopment of Africa by Europe,' *Africa, the arrival of Europeans and the trans-Atlantic slave,* Video available at: revealinghistories.org.uk/credits.html#WashingtonAlcott.

Alexei, B. & Keith, B. 2005. 'Sometimes a bumper crop is too much of a good thing,' *The New York Times*, 8 Dec 2005, USA.

Alpers, E. A. 1969. "Trade, State, and Society among the Yao in the Nineteenth Century," *The Journal of African History*, X (1969), 405–420.

AMCEN, 2011. *Addressing climate change Challenges in Africa: Practical Guide towards Sustainable Development*, African Union & AMCEN.

Asante, M. K. 2000. *The Egyptian philosophers: Ancient African voices from Imhotep to Akhenaten*, African American Images: Chicago.

Asante, M. K. 1990. *Kemet, Afrocentricity and knowledge*, Africana World Press: Trenton.

Asante, M.K. 1988. *Afrocentricity*, Trenton, NJ: Africa World Press.

Attwood, D. W. 2005. Big is ugly? How large-scale institutions prevent famines in Western India, *World Development* 33 (12): 2067-2083.

AU Conference of Ministers, 2008. *First session of the AU Conference of Ministers in charge of social development*, 27-31 October, Windhoek, Namibia.

Awolowo, B. 1961. *African unity*, Ibadan: Nigeria.

Ayittey, G. N. B. 1999. *Africa in Chaos*, St Martin's Griffin: New York.

Bafana, B. 18 June 2013. 'No till, more yields,' ReliefWeb, Available at: reliefwb.int/../no-till-more-yields/.

Bahl, K. 2016. "What are the advantages and disadvantages of globalisation?" *International Economics*, Quora.

Bain, R. 1937. *Technology and state government*, American Sociological Review 2 (Dec 1937), Washington DC: USA.

Bairoch, P. 1993. *Economics and world history: Myths and paradoxes*, University of Chicago Press, Chicago.

Balter, M. 2013. 'Farming was so nice, it was invented at least twice,' University of Tubingen.

Baran, P. 1973. *The political economy of growth*, Penguin: Harmondsworth.

Barfield, T. 1997. *The dictionary of anthropology*, Wiley-Blackwell: United Kingdom.

Barkin, D. 1997. *Food production, consumption, and policy, Encyclopaedia of Mexico*, Vol. 1, Fizroy Dearborn Publishers: Chicago.

Bartle, P. 1967. *The dependency syndrome,* Community Empowerment Collective: USA.

Batten, A. & Martina, A. 2005. *Diseases Dominate*, School of Economics: The Australian National University, Mimeo.

BBC, 17 February 2011a. Beneath the Surface: A Country of Two Nations
www.bbc.co.uk/history/british/victorians/bsurface_01.shtml.

BBC., 17 February 2011b. The British Presence in India in the 18th Century www.bbc.co.uk/history/british/empire_seapower/east_india_01.shtml.

Bello, W. 2003. 'Globalisation: The latest phase of imperialism,' Speech Presented to the One World on 10/07/2003, The Global South: India.

Bhattacharyya, S. 2007.Root causes of Africa's underdevelopment, *Working Paper in Economics and Development Studies,* Melbourne: Australia.

Bish, J. J. 2016. *Population growth in Africa: Grasping the scale of the challenge,* Population Media Centre, USA.

Bloom, D., and J. Sachs, J. 1998. Geography, Demography, and Economic Growth in Africa, *Brookings Papers on Economic Activity,* (2): 207-295.

Bodenheimer, S. 1970. *Dependency and imperialism: The roots of Latin American underdevelopment,* NACLA: New York.

Bonnel, R. 2000. HIV/AIDS and economic growth: A global perspective, *South African Journal of Economics* 68 (5): 820-855.

Boundless, 26 May 2016. 'Benefits of globalisation,' Boundless Management, Available at: https://www.boundless.com/management/textbooks/boundles-management-textbook/globalisation-and-business-14/globalisation-101/benefits-of-globalisation-470-3958.

Bradshaw, T. K. 2006. Theories of poverty and anti-poverty programs in community development, *RPRC Working Paper Number 06-05*, Rural Poverty Research Centre, Available Online at: http://www.rprconline.org.

Brereton, D. & Forbes, P. 2004. Monitoring the impact of mining on local communities: A hunter Valley Case study, CSRM: Available at: http://www.csrm.uq.edu.au/doc/Hunter_Valley.

Brundtland Commission. 1987. *Our common future,* World Commission on the Environment and Development: Oxford.

Business Dictionary, n.d. 'Environment,' Available at: BussinessDictionary.com

Carter, T. S. 1997. The failure of environmental regulation in New York: The role of co-option, corruption, and co-operative enforcement approach, *Crime, Law and Social Change* 26 (1): 27-52.

Centres for Disease Control and Prevention (CDC), 2016. *Environmental change*, U.S. Department of Health and Human Services: USA.

Chambers, R. 2004. *Ideas for development: Reflecting forwards,* IDS Working Paper 238, Institute of development studies, Sussex: England.

Chambua, S. E. 1994. 'The development debates and crisis of development theories: The case of Tanzania with special emphasis on peasants, state and capital,' In: Himmelstrand, U. *et al.* Eds. *Introduction to African perspectives on development: Controversies, dilemmas and openings,* James Currey: London.

Chawafambia, K. 6 October 2013. Zim maintains ban on GMOs, *Daily News*, Harare, Zimbabwe.

Chingwe, A. 27/06/2013. Reviving Zimbabwe's agriculture sector, *The Financial Gazette*: Harare.

Chisinga, B. 2010. 'Resurrecting the developmental state in Malawi,' In: Tambulasi, R. (Ed). *Reforming the Malawian public sector,* CODESRIA: Dakar.

Christie, F. & Halon, J. 2001. *Mozambique and the great flood of 2000*, Indiana University Press: Indiana.

Cliche, P. 2005. *A Reflection on the Concepts of "Poverty" and "Development,"* Canada: Canadian Catholic Organisation for Development and Peace.

Colman, D. & Nixson, F. 1994. *Economics of change in less developed countries*, Harvester Whetsheaf: New York.

Connelly, M. P. *et al.* 2000. *Feminism and development: Theoretical perspectives*, Oxford University Press: Oxford.

Cotter, J. 2003. *Troubled harvest: Agronomy and revolution in Mexico, 1880-2002*, Contributions in Latin American Studies no. 22, Praeger: Westport CT.

Dammania, R. *et al.* 2003. Trade liberalisation, corruption, and environmental policy formulation: Theory and evidence, *Journal of Environmental Economics and Management* 46 (3): 490-512.

Daniele, C. 2010. The limits of cultural globalisation? *Journal of Critical Globalisation Studies*, 3, p. 36–59.

Debasish (n.d). Major negative effects of population explosion, Available at: EconomicDiscussion.net.

De Beer, F. & Swanepoel, H. (Eds). 2000. *Introduction to development studies*, 2nd ed, Oxford University Press: Oxford.

De Castro, J. 1968a. *From Bandung to New Delhi: The Great Third World Crisis*, Revue Generale Belge, Brussels.

De Castro, J. 1968b. *Demographic explosion and hunger in the world*, Civillita delle Machine, Rome.

De Castro, J. 1970. Development strategy, *A paper presented during Environment and Society in Transition Conference,* New York: USA.

DeWeerdt, S. 2008. 'War and the environment,' World Watch: USA.

Dickson, D. 2006. "African science: Now is the time to deliver," SciDev.Net.

Dye, T. R. 1987. *Understanding public policy*, Engelwood Cliffs: New Jersey.

Dye, T. R. 2001. *Top-Down Policymaking*, Chatham House: New York.

Dos Santos, T. 1970. "The Structure of Dependence," *American Economic Review,* Vol. 60, p.231-236.

Easterlin, R. 1968. 'Overview on economic growth,' In: Sills, D. L. (Ed), *International Encyclopaedia of the social sciences*, Vol. 4, New York.

Easterly, W. 2008. *"Can the West save Africa?"* NBER Working paper no. 14363, September 2008.

Edelman, M. and Haugerud, A. (Eds.). 2005. *The Anthropology of Development and Globalisation: from Classical Political Economy to Contemporary Neoliberalism*, Malden, MA: Blackwell Publishers.

Ekwuru, G. 1999. *The pangs of an African culture in travail*, Totan Publishers Limited: Owerri.

Escobar, A. 1997. 'The Making and Unmaking of the Third World,' In: Majid Rahnema and Victoria Bawtree (Eds), *Post-Development Reader*, Sed Books: London.

Food and Agriculture Organisation of the United Nations, (FAO). 2008. *Climate change and food security: a framework document*, FAO: Rome.

FAO. 1948. 4th Session, Washington D.C, November 1948. Available at: http://www.fao.org.docrep/x5580E00.htm

Fei, J.C.H & Ranis, G. 1961. 'A theory of economic development', American Economic Review, 51:533-565. also in Eicher & Witt (Eds.), Agriculture in economic development.

Fisher, S. 2012. Challenges of climate change, Grantham Research Institute, The Guardian 27 Feb 2012.

Fischer, C. S. *et al.* 1996. *Inequality by design: Cracking the bell curve myth*, Princeton University Press: Princeton.

FitzGerald, P. *et al.* 1997. *Managing sustainable development in South Africa*, 2nd Ed, Oxford University Press: Oxford.

Frank, A. G. 1967. *Capitalism and underdevelopment in Latin America: Historical studies of Chile and Brazil*, Monthly Review Press: New York.

Frank, A. G. 2005. "The Development of Underdevelopment," Development: Critical Concepts in the Social Sciences: Washington DC.

Frank, A. G. 1998. *Reorient: Global economy in the Asian age*, Berkeley Press: UC.

Frank, A.G. *et al.* 1972. *Dependence and Underdevelopment in Latin America*: Anchor: New York.

Freire, P. 1970. *Pedagogy of the oppressed*, The Seabury Press: New York.

Friedman, T. L. 2005. "It's a Flat World, After All," New York Times Magazine; Apr 3, 2005.

Fukuyama, F. 1992. *The end of history and the last man*, Free Press: USA.

Fukuyama, F. 2002. *Our posthuman future: Consequences of the biotechnology revolution*, Farrar Straus and Giroux: USA.

Furtado, C. 1973. 'The Concept of External Dependence in the Study of Underdevelopment', in Wilber, C.K. (Ed.), *The Political Economy of Development and Underdevelopment*, Random House: New York.

Gallup, J. & Sachs, J. 2001. "The Economic Burden of Malaria," American Journal of Tropical Medicine and Hygiene, 64 (1-2): 85-96.

Gaud, W. 1968. 'Speech on Green Revolution: Accomplishments and apprehensions,' AgBioWorld, (8 March 1968).

Gemery, H. & Hogendorn, J. 1979. "The Economic Costs of West African Participation in the Atlantic Slave Trade: A Preliminary Sampling for the Eighteenth Century," In Gemery, H. and J. Hogendorn (Eds.). *The Uncommon Market: Essays in the Economic History of the Atlantic Slave Trade*, Academic Press: New York.

George, L. H. & Scott, R. 1980. *A Greek-English Lexicon,* Abridged Edn, Oxford University Press: UK.

Ghai, D. P. 1977. *The Basic Needs Approach to Development: Some Issues Regarding Concepts and Methodology,* Geneva: International Labour Office.

Gibbons, M. 2000. 'Universities and the new production of knowledge: Some policy implications for government,' In: Kraak, A. (Ed). *Changing modes: New knowledge production and its implications for higher education in South Africa,* HSRC: Pretoria.

Gore, C. 2000. The Rise and Fall of the Washington Consensus as a Paradigm for Developing Countries, *World Development*, 28 (5): 789–804.

Gosh, B. N. 2001. *Dependency Theory Revisited,* Ashgate Publishing: Burlington, Vermont.

Grace Communications Foundation. 2014. *Industrial crop production,* Food Programme: Grace Eco, Washington D. C.

Gundy, K. 1966.African explanations of underdevelopment: The theoretical basis for political action, The Review of Politics, 28 (1): 62-75.

Gwekwerere, R. 2000. Progress on the critical regional areas of concern, *Women in Development Southern African Awareness: A Gender and Development Newsletter for Southern Africa*, Issue No: 20. Available at: Widsaa/sardc.net.

Gyekye, K. 2013. *Philosophy, Culture and Vision: African Perspectives, Selected Essays,* Sub-Saharan Publishers: Accra.

Hai, S. 2012. 'Ghana to attract investment into bio-energy sector,' China.org.cn,Xinhua: China Internet Information Centre.

Hamdi, F. 2015.*The impact of globalisation in developing countries*, ICN Business School in France: France.

Hamid, S. & Craig, R. 1993. Religion: A confounding cultural element in the international harmonisation of accounting? *Abacus* 29 (2): 131-148.

Hardt, M. and Negri, A. 2000. *Empire*, Harvard University Press: Cambridge, MA.

Harris, J. M. 2000. Basic principles of sustainable development, Metford: Global Development and Environment Institute, *Working Paper No. 00-04*, Tufts University.

Hawthorne, W. 1999. "The production of slaves where there was no state: The Guinea-Bissau Region, 1450–1815," *Slavery & Abolition, XX* (1999), 97–124.

———, 2003. *Planting rice and harvesting Slaves: Transformations along the Guinea-Bissau Coast, 1400–1900,* Heinemann, Portsmouth, NH.

Hazell, P. B. R. 2009. The Asian Green Revolution, *IFPRI Discussion Paper*, International Food Policy Res Institute.

Held, D. *et al.* 1999. *Global Transformation: Politics, Economics and Culture*, Stanford University Press, Stanford: California.

Hellmuth, M. E., Moorhea, A. & Williams, J. 2007. *Climate risk management in Africa: learning from practice*, Silver Spring: IRI.

Hettne, B. 2002. Current Trends and Future Options in Development. In V. Desai & R.B. Potter (Eds.), *The Companion to Development Studies*. London: Arnold & New York: Oxford University Press.

Hobson, J. M. 2004. *The Eastern Origins of Western civilisation*, Cambridge University Press: Cambridge.

Human Development Report, 1996. Growth for human development: Overview, *United Nations Development Programme*, New York: USA.

Human Rights Watch. 27 July 2001. 'Old settlement farm, Marondera, Mashonaland East,' Human Rights Watch Interview.

Hyden, G. 1980. *Beyond Ujamaain Tanzania: Underdevelopment and an uncaptured peasantry*, Cambridge Press: London.

Hyden, G. 1983. *No short-cut to progress: African development in perspective*, Cambridge Press: London.

Ibrahim, M. (n.d). The effect of globalisation on the development of underdeveloped economies, *Mimeo, Central Bank of Nigeria*: Nigeria.

IMF Internal Review, 1997. *The ESAF at ten years: Economic Adjustment and Reform in low-income countries*, Occasional Paper no. 156, Dec 1997, Washington DC: USA.

Inikori, J. 1992. *The Chaining of a Continent: Export Demand for Captives and the History of Africa South of the Sahara, 1450-1870,* Institute of Social and Economic Research, University of the West Indies, Mona, Jamaica.

Isaacman, A. F. "The Countries of the Zambezi Basin," In: J.F.A. Ajayi, (Ed). *General history of Africa, VI*, Heinemann International, Paris.

Jacobsen, S. 2014. Sub Saharan Africa's underdevelopment, causes of it, and what the future might hold, *Master of Science in Strategy, Organisation and Leadership*, Aarhus School of Business and Social Sciences: Aarhus University.

Jagdish, B. 2004. *In defence of globalisation*, Oxford University Press: Oxford.

James, G. 1954. *Stolen legacy*, Africa World Press: New Jersey.

James, P. & Steger, M. B. 2014. A genealogy of globalisation: The career of a concept, *Globalisation 11* (4): 424-432.

Jennison, K. 2014. *Climate change offers business opportunities*, Environment Business International.

JLiddell, H. G. & Scott, R. 1980. *A Greek-English lexicon,* Oxford University Press: UK.

Jones, B. 2001. *Peacemaking in Rwanda: The dynamics of failure*, Boulder Publishers: Colorado.

Johnson, D. L. *et al.* 1997. Meanings of environmental change, *Journal of Environmental Quality*, 26: 581-589.

Jorgenson, D. 1961. 'The Development of a Dual Economy', *Economic Journal,* June 1961, pp. 309-334.

Kabeer, K. & Cook, S. 2000. *Re-visioning Social Policy in the South: Challenges and Concepts*, IDS Bulletin Vol. 31. (4).

Kaberuka, D. 2013. *Financing Africa's Development in the 21st Century*, AfDB: Washington.

Keeley, J. & Scoones, I. 1999. 'Understanding environmental policy processes: A review,' *IDS Working Paper 89*, IDS: Brighton.

Kendie, B. S. & Martens, P. 2008. 'Governance and sustainable development: An overview,' In Kendie, S. B. & Martens, P. (Eds), *Governance and sustainable development*, Marcel Hughes: Cape Coast, pp. 1-15.

Kenya Country Profile. 2007.*Library of Congress Federal Research Division*, Nairobi: Kenya.

Khosla, K. *et al.* 2004. *Gender and water*, IRC International Water and Sanitation Centre: The Netherlands.

Kimambo, I. N. 1989. The East African Coast and Hinterland, 1845–1880," in J.F.A. Ajayi, (Ed). *General History of Africa, VI*, Heinemann International, Paris.

Kitamura, J. 1969. Historical Roles of German Colonial Companies, *Keiei Shigaku: Japan Business History Review* 4 (2): 33-60.

Klein, Martin, 2001. The Slave Trade and Decentralized Societies, *Journal of African History*, XLII (2001), 49–65.

Kwinika, S. 4 August 2010. No more 'GMO' chickens from South Africa, *CFU News,* Harare: Zimbabwe, Available at: http://www.csmonitor.com.

Kyte, R. 2014. Climate change is a challenge for sustainable development, Guidar Forum 15 Jan 2014, Moscow: Russia.

Labica, G. 2007. 'From Imperialism to globalisation': In: Budgen, S. *et al.* (Eds.) *Lenin Reloaded*, pp. 222–38. Duke University Press: Durham, NC.

Lamb, D. 1983. *The Africans*, Random House: New York.

Lancaster, H. O. 1990. *Expectation of life: A study in the democracy, statistics and history of world mortality*, Springer-Verlag.

Landes, D. S. 1998. *The wealth and poverty of Nations,* Abacus books.

Larson, G. *et al.* 2014. Current perspectives and the future of domestication studies, *Proceedings of the National Academy of Sciences* 111 (17): 6139.

Lawal, G. 2006. Globalisation and development: The implications for the African economy, *Humanity & Social Sciences Journal 1* (1): 65-78.

League for the Fifth International Fighting for the Formation of a New World of Socialist Revolution (L5L). (01/11/2003). 'Globalisation: The latest stage of imperialism,' USA.

Lee, A. C.Y. (n.d). "Ancient Silk Road Travellers," *Silkroad Foundation*, Available at:Silk-road.com.

Lewellen, Ted C. 1995. *Dependency and Development: An Introduction to the Third World*, Westport, Connecticut: Bergin & Garvey.

Lewis, W.A. 1954. 'Economic development with unlimited supplies of labour', Manchester School, 22:139-191. also in Agarwala & Singh (Eds.), The economics of underdevelopment.

Lerner, D. 1968. 'Social aspects of modernisation,' In: Sills, D. L. (Ed), *International Encyclopedia of the social sciences*, Vol. 10, New York.

Mabogunje, A. 1980. *The development process: A spatial perspective*, Hutchinson & Company Publishers: South Africa.

MacPherson, S. 1982. *Social policy in the third world–the social dilemmas of underdevelopment*, Wheatsheaf Books: Brighton.

Made, J. 10 February 2016. GMO ban stays, *Zimbabwe News*, Harare: Zimbabwe.

Mahadi, A. 1992. "The aftermath of the Jihad in the central Sudan as a major factor in the volume of the Trans-Saharan Slave Trade in the Nineteenth Century," In: Elizabeth Savage, (Ed). *The uncommon market: Essays in the economic history of the Atlantic Slave Trade,* Frank Cass, London.

Makgoba, M. W. (Ed). 1999. *African renaissance: The new struggle*, Mafube Tafelberg: Cape Town.

Manning, P. 1983. Contours of Slavery and Social Change in Africa, *American Historical Review*, LXXXVIII (1983), 835–857.

———, 1990. *Slavery and African life*, Cambridge University Press: Cambridge, UK.

Mbajedwe, P. U. 2000. 'Africa and the Trans-Atlantic Slave Trade,' In: Toyin Falola, (Ed)., Africa Volume I: African History Before 1885, Carolina Academic Press, North Carolina.

Mark, O. 2012. 'Farming and machinery the South African way,' *Interview 14/09/2012*, Johannesburg: South Africa; Available at: www.fwi.co.uk/author/oliver-mark/.

Mawere, M. 2011. *Moral degeneration in contemporary Zimbabwean business practices*, Langaa Publishers: Bamenda.

Mawere, M. 2013. *Lyrics of reason and experience*, Langaa RPCIG Publishers: Bamenda.

Mawere, M. 2014a. *Divining the Future of Africa: Healing the Wounds, Restoring Dignity and Fostering Development*, Langaa RPCIG Publishers: Bamenda.

Mawere, M. 2014b. Western hegemony and conquest of Africa: Imperial hypocrisy and the invasion of African cultures, In: Mawere, M. & Mubaya R. T. (Eds). *African Cultures, Memory and Space: Living the Past Presence in Zimbabwean Heritage*, Langaa RPCIG Publishers: Bamenda.

Mawere, M. 2014c. *Culture, indigenous knowledge and development in Africa: Reviving interconnections for sustainable development*, Langaa Publishers: Bamenda.

Mawere, M. 2014d. *Environmental conservation through Ubuntu and other emerging perspectives*, Langaa Publishers: Bamenda.

Mawere, M. 2016. 'Colonial heritage, memory, and sustainability in dialogue: An introduction,' In: Mawere, M. & Mubaya, R. T. (Eds). *Colonial heritage, memory and sustainability in Africa: Challenges, opportunities and prospect*, Langaa RPCIG Publishers: Bamenda.

Mawere, M. 2015. *Humans, other beings and the environment: Harurwa (edible stinkbugs) and environmental conservation in south-eastern Zimbabwe*, Cambridge Publishers: Cambridge.

Mawere, M. 2011. Gold panning in central Mozambique: A critical investigation of the effects of gold panning in Manica Province, *International Journal of Politics and Good Governance*, 2 (2.4): 0976-1195.

Mawere, M. 2013. *Environment and Natural Resource Conservation And Management In Mozambique,* Langaa RPCIG Publishers: Bamenda.

Mawere, M. & Mubaya, T. 2016. *African philosophy and thought systems: A search for a culture and philosophy of belonging*, Langaa Publishers: Bamenda.

Mawere, M. & Nhemachena, A. 2013. Frantz Fanon in South Africa and Beyond: A Critical Review of Nigel Gibson's Fanonian Practices in South Africa, *The Journal of Pan African Studies* 6 (6): 225- 234.

Mawere, M. & Rambe, P. 2013. *Leveraging Educational Quality in Southern African Educational Systems: A Practitioners' Perspective,* Langaa RPCIG Publishers: Bamenda.

Manning, P. 1981. The Enslavement of Africans: A Demographic Model, *Canadian Journal of African Studies*, 15(3): 499-526.

Mbilinyi, M. 1992. 'Research methodologies in gender issues,' In: Meena, R. Ed. 1992. *Gender in Southern Africa: Conceptual and theoretical issues,* SAPES Books: Harare.

McCubbrey, D. 2016. *Negative and positive effects of globalisation for developing country business,* Business Fundamentals: Boundless.

Mcluhan, M. 1960. *Understanding media*, Gingko Press, Canada.

McManes, C. 2013. IEEE-USA Testifies in Favor of Green Card and U.S. Job Creation, retrieved 7 July 2016 from http://insight.ieeeusa.org/insight/content/ieeeusa/5875.

Meena, R. Ed. 1992. *Gender in Southern Africa: Conceptual and theoretical issues,* SAPES Books: Harare.

Mehta, S. M. 2001. *Population challenge and family welfare*, Anmol Publications Ltd: India.

Marger, 2008. *Social Inequality: Patterns and Processes*, McGraw Hill publishing.

Mkandawire, T. 2004. 'Disempowering New Democracies and the Persistence of Poverty,' In: *Globalisation, Poverty and Conflict*. Max Spoor ed. Dordrecht: Kluwer Academic Publishers, pp. 117-53.

Moore, D.S. 2005. *Suffering for Territory: Race, Place, and Power in Zimbabwe*, Weaver Press: Harare.

Moser, C. 1989. Gender planning in the third world; Meeting practical and strategic needs, *World Development* 17 (11): 1799-1825.

Moser, C. 1993. *Gender planning and development: Theory, practice and training*, Routledge: London.

Mowafi, M. (n.d). 'The meaning and measurement of poverty: A look into the global debate,' A paper Presented to the World Bank.

Moyo, D. 2009. *Dead Aid: why aid is not working and how there is a better way for Africa*, Farrar, Straus and Giroux.

Moyo, R. 7 June 2010. Zero tillage making a difference to Hurungwe farmers, The Zimbabwean, Harare.

Mrak, M. 2000. *Globalisation: Trends, challenges, opportunities for countries in transition*, United Nations Industrial Development Organisation: Vienna.

Musingafi, M. C. C. *et al.* 2013. *Gender dynamics: Development and peace studies perspectives*, International Institute for Science, Technology and Education (IISTE): New York.

Naiman, R. & Watkins, N. 1999. *A survey of the impacts of IMF Structural Adjustment in Africa: Growth, social spending and debt relief*, Centre for Economic and Policy Research: Washington DC.

Narayan, D. *et.al.,* 2000. *Voices of the Poor: Can Anyone Hear Us?* Oxford University Press: New York.

Nkwinti, G. 2012. Speech by the Minister of Rural Development and Land Reform, 2012 *Policy Speech*, Pretoria: South Africa.

Nyamnjoh, F. B. 2012a. Potted Plants in Greenhouses: A Critical Reflection on the Resilience of Colonial Education in Africa, *Journal of Asian and African Studies*, 47 (2): 129-154.

Nyamnjoh, F. B. 2012b. Blinded by Sight: Divining the Future of Anthropology in Africa, *Africa Spectrum*, 47, 2-3, 63-92.

Nyerere, J. 1968. *Freedom and Socialism: A Selection from Writings & Speeches, 1965-1967*, Oxford University Press: Oxford.Office of General Council, 2012. 'What is policy?' The University of Sydney: Sydney.

Obama, B. 2013. Remarks by President Obama at Young African Leaders Initiative Town Hall, retrieved 19 July 2016 from https://www.whitehouse.gov/the-press-office/2013/06/29/remarks-president-obama-young-african-leaders-initiative-town-hall.

OECD-FAO, 2013. 'OECD-FAO expect slower global agricultural production growth,' OECD, France.

Over, M. 1992. *The macro-economic impact of AIDS in sub-Saharan Africa*, Population and Human Resources Department: The World Bank.

O'Rourke, K. H. *et al*. 2000. When did globalisation begin? *NBER Working Paper*, No. 7632.

Patel, P. 2015. Immigrants Have a Growing Role in the U.S. Sci-Tech Workforce, 7 July 2016 from http://spectrum.ieee.org/tech-talk/at-work/education/immigrants-have-a-growing-role-in-the-us-scitech-workforce.

Payne, R. K. 2005. *Framework for understanding poverty*, Highlands, Texas: USA.

Peet, R. & Hartwick, E. 2009. *Theories of development: Connects, arguments, alternatives*, The Guliford Press: London.

Planas, F. 2012. *The exploitation of natural resources*, Un An Pour La Planete, Paris: France.

Plato, *The Republic*, Book 11, 369c.

Popay, J. *et al*. 2008. Understanding and tackling social exclusion, *Final Report to the WHO Commission on Social Determinants of Health From the Social Exclusion Knowledge Network*, UK.

Raftopoulos, B. 1998. *The Zimbabwe human development report*, Institute of Development Studies: Harare.

Ramlogan, R. 2004. *The Developing World and the Environment: Making the case for Effective Protection of the Global Environment*, University Press of America: New York.

Reyes, G. 2001. *Four main theories of development: Modernisation, dependency, world systems and globalisation*, University of Pitsburg: South Africa.

Riehl, S. 2013. 'Taming the wild: Millennia of cultivation at Chogha Golan in Iran turned wild wheat into domesticated wheat,' University of Tubingen.

Rispel, L. C. *et al.* 2009. Can Social Inclusion Policies Reduce Health Inequalities in Sub-Saharan Africa?—A Rapid Policy Appraisal, *Journal of Health Population and Nutrition,* 27(4): 492-504.

Rist, G. 1997. *The History of Development: From Western Origins to Global Faith* (Translated by Patrick Camiller), London & New York: Zed Books.

Robbins, P. 2000. The rotten institution: Corruption in natural resource management, *Political Geography* 19 (4): 423-443.

Robinson, W. I. 2004. *A Theory of Global Capitalism*, Johns Hopkins University Press: Baltimore, MD.

Rodney, W. 1970. *A History of the Upper Guinea Coast*, Clarendon Press, Oxford.

Rodney, W. 1972. *How Europe underdeveloped Africa*, Bogle-L'ouverture Publications: London.

Rostow, W. W. 1960. *The stages of economic growth: A non-communist manifesto*, Cambridge University Press: Cambridge.

Ruttan, V. 2002. Productivity growth in world agriculture: Sources and constraints, *Journal of Economic Perspectives* 16 (4): 161-184.

Sant'Ana, M. 2008. The Evolution of the Concept of Development: From Economic Growth to Human Development. *Democratic Governance and Theory of Collective Action, Sub-Network on Foreign Direct Investment and Human Development.*

Santos, B. D. S. *et al.* 2006. *The Rise of the Global left: The World Social Forum and Beyond.* London and New York: Zed Books.

Scalise, G., & Meredith, J. W. 2007. Letter to U.S. House of Representatives representatives Conyers, Smith, Lofgren, and

King, retrieved 7 July 2016 from http://www.ieeeusa.org/policy/policy/2007/101107.pdf.

Schipper, E. L. F. 2007. Climate change adaptation and development: Exploring the linkages, *Tyndall Working Paper 107*: UEA.

Scott, P. 1994. *The crisis of the university*, Croom Helm: London.

Seers, D. 1969. 'The Meaning of Development,' *International Development Review* 11(4): 2-6.

Seligson, Mitchell A. and John T. Passe-Smith. 1993. *Development and Underdevelopment: The Political Economy of Inequality,* Lynne Rienner Publishers: Colorado.

Sen, A. 1999. *Development as Freedom,* Oxford University Press: New York.

Shillington, K. 2012. 3rd Ed. *History of Africa*, Palgrave Macmillan: UK.

Shillington, K. 2002. *History of Southern Africa*, Palgrave Macmillan: UK.

Smith, A. 1776. *The Wealth of Nations,* Harmondsworth, UK: Penguin.

Smith, D. 2013. Robert Mugabe's land reform comes under fresh scrutiny, 10 May 2013, *The Guardian:* UK.

So, A. 1990. *Social Change and Development: Modernisation, Dependency, and the World System Theories,* Berkley, CA: Sage Publication.

Stoneman, C. 1981. Introduction. In C. Stoneman (Ed.), *Zimbabwe's Inheritance* (pp. 1-7), London and Basingstoke: The College Press (Pvt) Ltd.

Streeten, P., Burki, S., Ul Haq, M., Hicks, N. & Stewart, F. 1981. *First Things First: Meeting Basic Human Needs in the Developing Countries*. Published for the World Bank, New York and Oxford: Oxford University Press.

Ted, C. L. 1995. *Dependency and Development: An Introduction to the Third World,* Westport, Connecticut: Bergin & Gravey.

Teferra, D. 1997. Brain Drain of African Scholars and the Role of Studying in the United States, *International Higher Education*, 7: 4–8.

The Centers for Disease Control and Prevention (CDC), 2016. *Environmental change*, U.S. Department of Health and Human Services: USA.

Thomas, A. 2004. *The Study of Development*, Paper prepared for DSA Annual Conference, 6 November, Church House, London.

Todaro, M.P. 2000. *Economic Development* (7th Ed.), Reading, MASS: Addison-Wesley.

United Nations Development Programme (UNDP). 1990. *Human Development Report*, Oxford University Press: New York.

United Nations Development Programme (UNDP). 2000. Overcoming human poverty: UNDP Poverty Report 2000. Available at: http://www.undp.org/povertyreport.

UNDP. 2015. About Zimbabwe, *UNDP Around the World 2011-2015*, UNDP.

UN General Assembly Report, 1991. *Final review and appraisal of the implementation of the United Nations Programme of Action for African Economic Recovery Development*, 77th Plenary Meeting, 18 Dec 1991.

UN-HelpAge, 2003. *African Union/HelpAge International: Policy framework and plan of action on ageing*, HAI Africa Regional Development Centre, Nairobi.

UN-OHRLLS, 2001. *Criteria for identification and graduation of LDCs*, United Nations Office of the High Representative for the Least Developed Countries, Landlocked Developing Countries and the Small Island Developing Countries: UN.

UN-OHRLLS, 2015. *About LCDs A propos des pays les moins Avance*, United Nations Office of the High Representative for the Least Developed Countries, Landlocked Developing Countries and the Small Island Developing Countries: UN.

Seers, D. 1977. The new meaning of development, *International Development Review* no.3 (1977): 1- 8.

Seers, D. 1969. 'The Meaning of Development', *International Development Review*, 11 (4): 2-6.

Sen, A. 1999. *Development as freedom*, Random House: New York.

Sen, G. & Grown, C. 1987. *Development, crisis, and alternative versions: Third world women's perspectives,* Monthly Review Press: New York.

Shwayder, M. 2013. Poorest of the poor: United Nations Report on World's 'Least Developed Countries,' 19/03/2013, Reuters.

Smith, A. 1776. *Wealth of nations*, Modern Library Edition: New York.

South Africa Yearbook 2014/2015. *Government communications*, Department of Government Communications and Information System, South Africa.

Stiff, P. 2000. *Cry Zimbabwe: Independence – Twenty years on*, Galago Publishing: South Africa.

Stiglitz, J. 2002. *Globalisation and its discontents*, W. W Norton: USA.

Swanepoel, H. 2011. 'Introduction': In De Beer, F. & Swanepoel, H. (Ed.), *Introduction to development studies,* Oxford University Press: Oxford.

Takagi, Y. 1972. On a development theory of a dual economy, *Paper Presented to the School of Economics, August 1972,* Kyoto University: Japan.

The Economist, 2000. 'Africa a hopeless continent,' *The Economist Newspaper, 31 May 2000*, Washington DC: USA.

Theron, D. 2005. 'Public participation as a micro-level development strategy', In: Davids, I. *et al* (Eds), *Participatory development in South Africa: A development management perspective,* Van Schaik Publishers.

Thomas, A. 2004. 'The study of development,' *Paper Prepared for DSA Annual Conference,* 6 November, Church House: London.

Tilman, D. *et al.* 2002. Agricultural sustainability and intensive production practices, *Nature* 418 (6898): 671-7.

The Indian Express, 1950. 'Rust-resistant wheat varieties: Work at Pusa Institute,' 7 February 1950, India.

Third World Economics Trends & Analysis No. 168 1-15 September, 1997.

Todaro, M. P. 1992. *Economics for a developing world: An introduction to principles, problems and policies for development*, 3rd Ed, Longman: New York.

Toure, S. 1962. Africa's future and the world, *Foreign Affairs, XLI* (October 1962): 145- 146.

Toure, S. 1959. *Toward full re-Africanisation: Policy and principles of the Guinean Democratic Party*, Paris: France.

Valentine, C. A. 1968. *Culture and Poverty,* University of Chicago: London.

Van der Warf, H. & Petit, J. 2002. Evaluation of the environmental impact of agriculture at the farm level: A comparison and analysis of 12 indicator-based methods, *Agriculture, Ecosystems and Environment* 93 (1-3): 131-145.

Vansina, J. 1966. *Kingdoms of the Savanna*, University of Wisconsin Press, Madison.

Vincent, P. 1995. *End of ideology?*, Earth Sciences: Washington DC.

Viner, J. n.d. Cited in Guru, S. 'What is the meaning of underdevelopment?' *Economics*, The Next Generation Library.

Walker, C., with Institute for Poverty, Land and Agrarian Studies (PLAAS). (July 13, 2013). The Distribution of Land in South Africa: An Overview, Article available at PLAAS website: http://www.plaas.org.za/sites/default/files/publications.pdf/No1%20Fact%20check%20web.pdf

Waller-Hunter, J. & Jones, T. 2002. Globalisation and sustainable development, *International Review for Environmental Strategies,* 3 (1): 53-62.

Wallerstein, I. 1974. *The modern world-system 1: Capitalist agriculture and the origins of the European world-economy in the 16th Century*, Academic Press: New York.

Wax, D. D. 1973. Preferences for Slaves in Colonial America, *Journal of Negro History*, LVIII (1973), 371–401.

Wetmore, S. B. & Theron, F. 1998. Community development and research: Participatory learning and action-a development strategy in itself, *Development Southern Africa* 15 (1): 29-54.

World Bank. 1980. *World Development Report 1980*, Washington: World Bank.

World Bank. 2008. Making development climate change resilient, A World Bank Strategy for sub-Saharan Africa, Washington D.C: USA.

World Health Organisation, 2006. *The health of the people: The African regional health report*, Regional Office for Africa, World Health Organisation: Geneva.

Worldwatch Institute. 2013. 'Modern warfare causes unprecedented environmental damage,' Worldwatch Institute: Washington D.C. Available at: worldwatch@worldwatch.org.

World Migration. 2008. *Managing Labour Mobility in the Evolving Global Economy*, Volume 4 of IOM World Migration Report Series: International Organisation for Migration.

WTTC. 2013. Travel and tourism economic impact 2013 South Africa, *World Travel and Tourism Council*, Johannesburg: South Africa.

Yaman, S. 2001. 'Historical development of globalisation,' Available at: http://w3.qazi.edu.tr/web/syaman/kuressellesmen2.htm; Retrieved on: 26/04/2016.

Zimbabwe's Ministry of Finance and Economic Development. 2014. *Poverty datum lines – January 2014*, Harare: Zimbabwe. Available at: www.zimtreasury.gov.zw; Retrieved on: 21/08/2016.

Zineldin, M. 2002. Globalisation, strategic cooperation and economic integration among Islamic/Arab countries, *Management Research Review* 25(4): 35-61.

Zivenge, W. 2016. 'Globalisation and development in Africa,' *Lecture Notes on the 12/04/2016*, Law School, Great Zimbabwe University.

www.ingramcontent.com/pod-product-compliance
Lightning Source LLC
LaVergne TN
LVHW020346260326
834688LV00045B/1553